Cooking
With Family & Friends

A collection of our favorite recipes

Susan C. Furci

Express Image Books

Express Image Books: http://www.barbarasanders.com

All Express Image titles, imprints and distributed lines are available at special quantity discounts for bulk purchases for sales promotion, premiums, fund-raising, educational or institutional use.

Express Image and logos Reg. U.S. Pat. & TM Office

ISBN 13: 9781479274055

ISBN 10: 1479274054

First Printing: September 2012

Printed in the United States of America

Dedication

With deep appreciation and admiration to my wonderful husband, Don aka Doc. Thank you for allowing me to be myself all these years and to fulfill the gifts that God gave me.

Thank you for providing a beautiful home where our family lives with laughter, love and peace. For loving God with all your heart and then loving us and showing us how important it is to say, "I'm sorry, please forgive me."

I thank God for giving us this loving family and for the times we share around food, laughter and fellowship.

Thank you to our wonderful grown children who have blessed our lives abundantly and made parenting look easy! How fortunate we are to live close by and to be a part of your lives on a regular basis.

May this lifelong collection of these favorite recipes be an inspiration to you and your children to keep our family traditions for many years. And thanks for giving us the most precious gifts, our wonderful grandchildren; Bailey, Abigail, Brady, Tyler, Aiden, Lucia, Sophia, and Giada. May you always look back and remember all the fun you had with Mimi and Papa and know how much we love you.

May they remind you of how very important each of you are in our family circle and may you never say, "I sure wish Mom would have written down that recipe!"

Live simply, love generously, care deeply, speak kindly, walk tenderly and then, leave the rest to God ~ Monsignor Anthony Borrelli

Introduction and Acknowledgements

Over the years many people walk in and out of our lives but some people make imprints that are everlasting...that's my friend, Barbara Sanders.

Barbara, the photographer (she was there for our babies coming home from the hospital, birthdays and countless photos ops), ballerina, ceramic teacher (one Christmas I made all my holiday gift money selling the ceramics that she fired for me), potter, music composer, pastor's wife (excellent counselor) writer and now author—you name it, she's done it. She's written two novels! But, in the early years she wrote mostly letters, and actually, that's where our story began....

A long time ago, during a rather stressful time in my early years of marriage, our husbands met. Doc and Daryl really hit it off, but I was in no mood to go through the painstaking process of making another friend, (just too much work). However, I did agree to meet Daryl and Barbara over dinner. The next day, I found a very lengthy letter on my front porch encouraging me to "hang in there." Our stories were similar, as she had been through many of the same trials I was enduring. Her sincere and heartfelt letter, about eight pages long (I often tease that it was probably 84-pages!) let me know that they too had muddled through some really tough times. Her Godly wisdom and down-to-earth encouragement caused me to rethink whether I wanted to spend the time getting to know her. I now consider this as one of my best decisions because Barbara has surely been a shining light in my life. Not to mention tons of fun! If I had to find one major flaw in her character it would be her lack of interest in football even though she married an NFL offensive tackle!

Recently, Barbara and I had the opportunity to spend some time together at our home in Ohio. During that stay, I proudly showed her my three ring binder filled with years of recipes that I had organized, a couple of years earlier, during my recuperation from knee replacement surgery. I was so proud of this labor of love that I could pass to our grown children. She took one look at the collection and immediately wanted to make copies. She's always encouraged me to write and in the past few years I started putting personal thoughts down and found it very rewarding. She, on the other hand, has written several books. Barbara's memoir entitled, "Puttin' On the Dog & Gettin' Bit," is written in the witty style of Erma Bombeck, and it contains some of our infamous family stories. She's put those "tidbit" stories in the back of this book. What fun we have had putting this together! Fortunately, I had part of this recipe file stored in my computer, so off she ran producing this cookbook. This project was blessed to have a computer expert on board who programmed the index of recipes and helped us out of many jams. Thanks, Anthony! Carol, Josh and Lena, thanks so much for your proof-reading efforts.

As I think about the many people who have shared their recipes with me, it's overwhelming. Certainly, I could never begin to remember all the wonderful cooks who said "yes" when I paid them the ultimate compliment of asking, "Can I have your recipe?" Therefore, this cookbook is not solely mine, but is lovingly honored with all those who are represented in it. My heart is filled with gratitude to all of my friends, family members and acquaintances that have blessed my life by sharing with me their homemade recipes.

I thank God for trusting me with the gift of hospitality and allowing me to spend many hours serving. I thank my mother for entrusting kitchen duties to me when I was hardly tall enough to reach the counter. I hope that I will always welcome my grandchildren into my domain and not forget that a mess is easier to mend that a broken spirit.

It is my hope that you will find many delicious (and often easy to prepare) dishes to share with your family. And while you're at it, have a laugh or two.

God bless you!   Susan Furci

In love of the brothers be tenderly affectionate one to another; in honor preferring one another... contributing to the needs of the saints; given to hospitality. Romans 12: 10-13

Please feel free to email me and let me know how much you enjoy this cookbook. If you do write, please put "cookbook" in the subject line. I would love to hear from you!

Furcimom@aol.com

There is one thing more exasperating than a wife who can cook and won't, and that's a wife who can't and will. ~ Robert Frost

Contents

Susan's disclaimer:

Any original recipe presented to me is subject to my personal changes.

The first time I prepare a dish, I return to the written recipe and make notes. Therefore, the next time I prepare it, I might add or subtract a little of an ingredient to conform to our liking. But once I feel like the recipe is perfected, I stick with it.

In my kitchen you'll always see me following my recipes to the tee. Recently, a friend asked why. To which, I replied, "If my guests (including family) remember a dish that I served that they loved, I want that dish to be just as good the second time as it was the first." I call this process tweaking.

So, if you see your recipe in this book and it's slightly different, please forgive me…you've been tweaked!

In preparing this cookbook I've gotten lots of input, questions and suggestions. Therefore, at the end of the recipe section are my "helpful hints," which is a list of suggestions that might be new to you or maybe not….

I've added spaces for written notes. I hope every cook using these recipes will make notes, as I do, for each new recipe.

Appetizers

Notes

Oda's Dried Beef Log

Using an electric mixer blend:
2 packages of cream cheese softened (8 oz.)
1 package dried chip beef-diced into tiny pieces
1 T. Worcestershire
1 T. Accent brand seasoned salt
Fold in:
Diced green onions (4 or 5)
Form a log or ball and wrap in plastic wrap to store.
Option: roll in chopped walnuts.
Serve with your favorite crackers

Dr. Bill Burke's Artichoke Dip
Super easy and super tasty!

1 glass jar of artichokes (6 oz.) drained and chopped
1 cup mayonnaise
1 cup dry grated Parmesan Cheese
Garlic powder, salt and crushed red pepper to taste.
Place mixture in a glass pie plate. Bake in 350-degree oven
until bubbly or microwave until hot. Serve with crackers.

Mariann's Cowboy Caviar

1 Can white beans (drained)
1 Can black beans (drained)
1 cup olive oil
2 T. fresh garlic, minced
4 chopped green onions (about an 8 inch long piece)
2 T. Dijon mustard
¼ cup red wine vinegar
Mix well. Serve with favorite crackers.

Joel's Smoked Salmon Spread
If you like salmon, you'll love this!

1 package of smoked salmon (8 oz.)
12 ounces softened cream cheese
Juice from ½ lemon
Dill weed to taste
Work salmon and cream cheese with fork until spreadable, add lemon and dill. Place in bowl alongside rye or pumpernickel party breads, offering capers, diced onions, and diced tomatoes.

Mozzarella Caprese
With French bread we sometimes make a meal out of this!

Sliced tomatoes
Fresh mozzarella cheese
Garlic crushed or minced
Basil leaves use whole or cut into thin slices (this is done by rolling several fresh basil leaves into a small cylinder and using scissors to cut into small strips)
Thinly sliced onion, sweet or purple
Olive oil
Balsamic vinegar
Susan's Italian salad dressing (see page 47)
Salt and pepper

We love tomatoes and we love fresh Mozzarella cheese, so this is a dish you will find on our table all year long. The variations are many so take your pick and serve it for company or yourselves. Slice the tomatoes and cheese then arrange them on a platter and add any of the above ingredients, making it your own version.

Betty's Deviled Eggs

Boil eggs (10 minutes), peel and cut into halves long ways. Mash and mix yellow centers with sweet pickle relish, salt, granulated garlic and mayonnaise to taste. Spoon the creamy mixture into the halved eggs. Sprinkle with paprika.

Easy Appetizer Meatballs
This is so easy but delicious!

1 bag frozen Italian cooked meatballs (thawed)
1 bottle chili sauce and 1 small bottle grape jelly (6 oz.)

Mix jelly and chili sauce in a stovetop pan to dissolve jelly, blend well. Put meatballs in a casserole dish and pour sauce over it. Bake about 45 minutes at 350 degrees until heated. Can use crock-pot also.

Artichoke Dip

1 jar artichokes (14 oz. size)
2 packages of crumbled feta cheese
1 cup mayonnaise
½ cup Parmesan cheese
1 jar pimentos (optional)
1 crushed clove of garlic
Place in glass dish and bake at 350 degrees for 20-25 minutes.

Some people like to paint pictures, or do gardening, or build a boat in the basement. Other people get a tremendous pleasure out of the kitchen, because cooking is just as creative and imaginative an activity as drawing, or woodcarving, or music. ~ Julia Child

Chicken Egg Rolls by Inga
International Party

1 package of egg roll wrappers
4 chicken breasts with bone and skin for extra flavor
3 large carrots, chopped
2 cups chopped celery
½ head of cabbage, chopped
2 cloves of garlic, minced
½ cup soy sauce
1 ½ cup reserved chicken broth
1 T. butter
Salt and pepper

Boil chicken in salt and pepper water, saving broth for later. Cool chicken, skin and debone. Sauté onion and garlic in the butter. Add soy sauce, carrots, celery and cook until tender. Add 1½ cups of broth (from cooked chicken) to the cabbage for another 5 minutes *(don't overcook the cabbage)*. Drain well. Add shredded chicken and mix. Roll into wrappers sealing edges with raw egg. Deep fry or pan fry in hot oil. Serve with traditional egg roll sauces.

Mexican Dip ala Cousin Jana

Use 9x13 dish or flat round tray
Cover bottom with layer of refried beans
Layer 8 oz. cream cheese with 1 package taco seasoning
Layer in no certain order:
Tomatoes, black beans (rinsed), chopped green onions, 3 avocados (mashed with a little sour cream) top with shredded sharp cheddar cheese, and sliced black olives.
Optional: jalapeños, taco meat, crushed red pepper
Serve with Scoops brand chips and salsa on the side.

Liz's Bite Size Tacos

1 lb ground beef
1 package taco seasoning mix
2 cups of French's fried onions crushed
¼ cup chopped fresh cilantro
½ t. crushed red pepper
32 bite size round tortilla chips (Scoops)
1 cup shredded sharp cheddar cheese
¾ cup sour cream

Cook beef in non-stick skillet over medium heat until browned, drain fat. Stir in taco seasoning mix, ¾ cup water, 1 cup crunched fried onions and cilantro. Simmer 5 minutes stirring often.

Preheat oven to 350 degrees. Arrange tortilla chips on a foil lined baking sheet. Spoon in beef mixture, sour cream and top with remaining onions and cheese.

Bake for 5 minutes or until cheese is melted and onions are golden.

Dipping Oil

Many times I use this instead of butter with Italian bread.

½ to ¾ cup olive oil
2 cloves crushed garlic
1 t. granulated garlic
½ t. oregano
4-5 leaves fresh basil (minced)
½ t. dried parsley
Salt and a pinch of red pepper
Combine the above ingredients and put in a flat bowl to share while dipping your favorite bread.

Asparagus Wrapped in Prosciutto

This appetizer will wow your guests. Wrapping maybe a little difficult at first, but don't give up.

Use fresh asparagus spears (medium size) cut off the bottom so what is left is about 8-10 inches long rinse and dry.
Buy prosciutto (Italian Ham) from your deli or grocery
Cut the prosciutto in half lengthwise so that you have a strip that is approximately 8-10 inches long by 2 inches wide (I use scissors)
Place the asparagus on the prosciutto and roll it to cover the stalk almost to the end. Wrap the meat tightly around the spear (like you would wrap a ribbon around a pencil)
Place on a baking sheet, no need for oil, because the meat has a little fat around it
Bake at 375 degrees for 8-10 minutes
The larger the spear the longer you will bake it
You want it to be crisp (so don't overcook) so you can pick up the spear and eat it with your fingers

When making this for guests I always include a few spears that do not have the ham, just in case one of my guests may not eat ham.

Asparagus with Sea Salt

Wonderful as an appetizer or a veggie

Wash and remove bottom of asparagus spears
Place asparagus spears on the baking sheet
Sprinkle with sea salt
Drizzle with olive oil
Bake at 375 degrees for 6-10 minutes depending on the size of the asparagus.

Tomato Canapés Ala Bonnie

These are so delicate and tasty, what a nice addition to any appetizer buffet!

¾ cup finely diced tomatoes
2 t. finely diced onions
1 t. finely chopped fresh basil leaves
⅛ t. granulated garlic
Salt and pepper to taste
1 package mini Phyllo shells
½ cup packed shredded mozzarella cheese
¼ cup mayo
4 T. real bacon pieces

Preheat oven to 350 degrees.
Place diced tomatoes in a colander. Sprinkle with onion, basil and seasonings. Toss to coat. Allow to drain, stirring occasionally.

Fill each Phyllo shell with a scant tablespoon of the tomato mixture. Stir together the cheese and mayo. Frost the top of each shell with a scant tablespoon of the cheese mixture. Sprinkle each shell with small amount of the bacon pieces Bake the filled shells for 10-12 minutes. Serve hot.

Be hospitable to one another without grumbling. As each has received a gift, employ it in serving one another, as good managers of the grace of God...I Peter 4:8

Veggie Dip I

Combine 8 oz. mayonnaise and 8 oz. sour cream
Add:
1 t. of the following:
Garlic powder, Lawry's seasoned salt, dill weed, parsley, dried onion flakes.
2 Drops of Tabasco. Serve with fresh vegetables.

Veggie Dip II

1 cup mayonnaise
Combine: Juice from ½ lemon add 2 cloves crushed garlic
1 package cream cheese (8 oz.) softened
½ tube anchovy paste
4 whole green onion with tops, chopped
Mix together and chill before serving.

Veggie Dip III

2 packages of 8 oz cream cheese, softened
2 cups of mayonnaise
1 small onion minced
½ t. granulated garlic
2 heaping tablespoons of minced horseradish
Salt and pepper to taste
Blend with mixer.

Can never get enough dip recipes!

Vicki's Yummy Ham Sandwiches

Ingredients:
2 packages of Kings Hawaiian mini rolls split in half.
1 lb. of shredded deli style ham
½ lb. of shredded Swiss cheese

Spray a 9 x 13 glass pan and place bottom-half of rolls in pan (it will be tight).

Dressing:
½-¾ cup of melted butter
1 ½ T. Poppy seed salad dressing
1 ½ T. Dijon mustard
2 T. dried onion flakes
1 ½ t. Worcestershire sauce

Spread sauce over the bottom layer of rolls, reserve a small amount to brush on the top of rolls before baking. Beginning with the shredded ham, layer the bottom rolls, ending with the shredded cheese. Place the tops of the rolls on top of the cheese. Brush with the remaining dressing and bake at 350 degrees for 12-15 minutes or until the cheese melts. Slice into mini sandwiches before serving.

Great for football weekend parties! Naturally, we are Ohio State University "Buckeye" fans! Recently, our biking friends, Jack & Vicki, invited my brother, John and I to watch an OSU VS. PURDUE football game with them. I don't remember who won the game, but I sure do remember these delicious mini sandwiches! There's nothing like a football Saturday shared with good friends!

Rumaki

3 cans whole water chestnuts
1 lb. bacon (cut each slice into half-size pieces)
Wrap bacon around water chestnuts and secure with toothpick
Bake at 275 degrees for 1 hour…drain grease

Combine:
⅔ cup ketchup
1 cup sugar
Pour sauce over Rumaki
Bake at 275 degrees for about 1 hour or until done.

I've tried numerous Rumaki recipes, but this one is the best!

Guacamole

4 avocados, peeled
3 hardboiled eggs
1 small onion finely chopped
½ t. Tabasco sauce and 2 T. chili sauce
Granulated garlic to taste
1 T. lemon juice
Lawry's brand seasoned salt and pepper to taste
Blend above ingredients together and serve with your favorite corn chips or Simply Naked Chips

Do not neglect to show hospitality to strangers, for thereby some have entertained angels unawares. ~ Apostle Paul

Mimi's Sausage Rolls

Ingredients:
1 lb Bob Evans sausage can use mild or hot or half of each
½ lb grated Swiss cheese
½ lb grated Monterey jack cheese
By grating the cheese it takes less time to for it to melt
3 large cloves minced or pressed garlic
1 t. granulated garlic *(see my hints in back of book)*
Crushed hot pepper (optional)
Flour tortillas
Jar of salsa *(in the early years I made homemade, now it's in the jar)*
Sometimes I add chopped onions to jarred salsa.

Brown sausage, when halfway cooked, add both kinds of garlic and crushed red pepper (if desired)
Always drain off as much fat as you can.
In a large skillet, wok or microwave combine the cheeses and let melt over low heat, being careful not to burn the cheese.
When melted, fold in sausage mixture
Microwave tortillas. Place a paper towel between each tortilla and place in microwave to heat.
Spoon a generous amount of cheese/sausage mixture on the tortilla like you are making a burrito. Top with a large spoonful of salsa (optional). Roll tortilla tucking in the bottom so the juice doesn't run out.

This dish came to me after going to "Carlos and Charlie's" restaurant in Acapulco, Mexico on our honeymoon. We loved this appetizer so much, that upon returning from vacation, I hustled to the grocery to try to find the ingredients that I suspected were in it. To this day I'm not sure how close it is to the original dish but family and friends have enjoyed it for years. My beloved neighbors, Hunter and Taylor Oda gave it the name.

Mexican Layered Salad

3 to 5 ripe Avocados, mashed with juice of ½ lemon
½ t. salt
1 can green chili salsa (the hotter the better)
1 medium red onion, chopped
1 can pitted black olives
2 medium tomatoes, chopped
½ lb. shredded cheddar cheese
½ lb. shredded Monterey jack cheese

Layer ingredients in an 8 x 12 deep glass pan. *I usually start with the cheeses then salsa, onions, olives, tomatoes and last the avocados. Putting the seed of the avocado in the middle of the top of the dish will prevent it from turning brown.*
Serve with corn chips.

Lena's Salsa

Combine:
2 cans Delmonte brand diced tomatoes with green chilies
1 can Delmonte brand diced tomatoes with garlic/basil
½ cup cilantro
3 cloves of garlic, minced
½ sweet onion
½ white onion
3 green onions chopped
1 red bell pepper
½ yellow and ½ orange bell pepper
3 jalapenos, deseeded,
1 - 4 chipotle peppers in adobe sauce, deseeded…*depends on how spicy you like it. I usually scoop some adobe sauce from the can in the salsa.* Blend all together and enjoy!

Lena's Yummy Hummus

Combine:
1 can chick peas
½ cup tahini
1 ½ T. minced garlic
1 t. salt
½ t. cumin
⅛ cup lemon juice
⅛ cup water…optional
¼ cup olive oil
Blend all ingredients together and enjoy.

*Many times I make a double recipe because it's so good
and will last in refrigerator for a few days.*

Beth's White Corn Salsa

In a large bowl, dice the following: 1 red, 1 yellow and 1
orange pepper. Green pepper (optional)
½ red or sweet onion, diced
3 green onions, cut up, use some of the green stems
3 large tomatoes, diced
1-2 can sweet white corn (rinse and drain)
1-2 can black beans, or garbanzos (rinse and drain)
1-2 cloves garlic minced or pressed
Salt and pepper
Options: cilantro, artichokes, jalapenos, cumin, pineapple

Dressing:
3 T. each of Sherry vinegar and honey
¼ cup Good Seasons bottled salad dressing
3 T. lime juice.
*I have seen this recipe using only lime juice for the
dressing personally I like my dressing.*

Cheese Puffs – (called tyropita)
This yummy appetizer is served at the Greek Festival.

Filling:
1 package of cream cheese (3 oz.) softened
1 cup grated provolone cheese (or any sharp cheese)
1 egg
Mix together and set aside.
Dough:
Athens Strudel Leaves (thaw according to directions)
Butter counter before starting and use damp towel to cover
dough to keep leaves from drying out while working.
Use 2 sheets at a time. Butter each leaf using plenty of
melted butter. Place 1 teaspoon filling on strip of dough
about 1 ½ inches wide, fold in triangle to the end. *WORK
QUICKLY*
Bake at 350 degrees for 20-25 minutes. Can be frozen
before baking. *This is the recipe we were making in the
chapter entitled "The Stork's Surprise Visit." Pg.183*

Crabmeat Spread

6 oz. crab meat (thaw and drain) or use fresh
8 oz. cream cheese (room temperature)
2 t. horseradish
Finely chopped onion
Salt, pepper and crushed red pepper to taste.

Suzanne's Wonderful Dip

In glass casserole layer: Cream Cheese (2 packages of 8
oz.) room temperature, 2 Cans Hormel Turkey Chili ("No
Beans") sprinkle granulated garlic and crushed red pepper
to taste. Top with lots of sharp Cheddar cheese and
microwave until cheese is melted. Serve with corn chips.

Cheesy Artichoke Squares

Been showing up on every buffet table of mine for years

Combine:
4 eggs, well beaten
¼ cup Italian dry bread crumbs
½ t. salt, ⅛ t. pepper, ½ t. oregano, ½ t. crushed red pepper
set aside
Sauté: ½ cup finely chopped onion
2 cloves garlic, finely chopped
2 T. butter
Remove from heat and add:
2 cups Cheddar cheese
2 6 oz. jars marinated artichokes (drained and chopped)
Combine egg with crumb mixture. Spread into greased
11x7 ½ inch glass baking dish. Bake at 350 degrees for 30
minutes Cut into 1-inch squares. Serve hot or cold.

Bruschetta

For a real treat to go with any Italian meal

1 loaf French or Italian bread cut in narrow rounds
Cut fresh tomatoes into small pieces. (*I like plum tomatoes
for this*)
Use *small* amount of *minced* onion...*this is tricky...if you
use too much it will over power all the other tastes. I would
suggest starting with a tablespoon; add more to your taste.*
1 small clove pressed garlic, salt and pepper to taste with 3
to 4 leaves of fresh basil (minced)
Place bread rounds on cookie sheet and spread lightly with
garlic butter. Toast under broiler, remove from oven, turn
rounds over and sprinkle with finely grated Parmesan
cheese and return to oven to toast the 2nd side.
Serve tomatoes in a bowl surrounded by the garlic toasts.

Perfect Guacamole

This is a spicier version of one of our favorite appetizers.

2 ripe avocados
½ red onion, minced
1-2 Serrano chilies…*or a squeeze of chili paste (easier)*
1 T. limejuice
½ t. coarse salt
Dash of pepper
½ ripe tomato or tablespoons of Salsa
Several drops of Buffalo hot sauce.

Mash avocados, mix ingredients together then mix with mashed avocados
Serve with blue corn chips

Warren's Easy Excellent Guacamole
International Party

6 ripe avocados (mashed)
Juice from two limes
Diced yellow onion
Salt to taste
Goes well with Simply Naked chips

I know this looks too simple to be great, but it is a fabulous and easy twist on guacamole. The lime makes this dish!

This is my invariable advice to people: Learn how to cook – try new recipes, learn from your mistakes, be fearless, and above all have fun! ~ Julia Child

Soups

Notes

Pasta Bean Minestrone

4 ripe tomatoes, quartered
5 cups chicken stock
1 T. olive oil
2 onions
3 stalks celery
4 strips of raw bacon, chopped into small pieces
1 can ready cooked Navy beans (Great Northern, 10 oz.)
1 package of soup pasta (5 oz.)
Salt and pepper to taste
1 cup fresh basil

Place tomatoes in 2 cups of chicken stock in a blender and puree until smooth. Set aside. Heat a large saucepan over medium to high heat. Add the oil, onions, celery, and bacon bits for 8 minutes or until the onions are soft. Add the tomato mixture, remaining stock and beans to the pan and simmer for another 12 minutes. Add the soup pasta and continue cooking until the pasta is done. Stir basil and serve.

"Do you have a kinder, more adaptable friend in the food world than soup? Who soothes you when you are ill? Who refuses to leave you when you are impoverished and stretches its resources to give a hearty sustenance and cheer? Who warms you in the winter and cools you in the summer? Yet who also is capable of doing honor to your richest table and impressing your most demanding guests? Soup does its loyal best, no matter what undignified conditions are imposed upon it. You don't catch steak hanging around when you're poor and sick, do you?
~ Judith Martin (Miss Manners)

White Chili

48 ounces Northern Beans in a glass jar
16 ounces mild salsa
2 Jalapeno peppers, chopped
2 garlic cloves, minced or pressed
1 ½ lbs. boneless chicken
3 cups chicken broth
½ lb. Monterey Jack cheese
2 t. cumin
Cut chicken into bite size chunks and brown in very little oil. Add garlic, cumin, and peppers. Add chicken broth, salsa, and beans and bring to a boil. Simmer for 20 minutes, add cheese and enjoy!

Heidi, daughter number one, has taught me to make a leaner and healthier dish as the years have gone by. But don't miss my mom's red chili ala Beth…as it's wonderful too.

Stracciatella Soup
Make this with bruschetta and you have a delicious and easy meal.

Heat in large saucepan:
1 carton chicken broth (32 oz.)
3 T. fresh parsley (chopped)
1 can chicken breast (13oz.)
½ cup pastina or other small soup pasta
½ cup water
Salt and pepper to taste
Beat together:
2 eggs
½ cup Parmesan cheese
When pasta is cooked drop egg mixture by spoonful into hot broth, until egg is completely cooked.

Beth's Chili

Ingredients:
3 lbs. ground beef
1 large onion, chopped
2 cans crushed tomatoes (28 oz. each)
2 cans tomato sauce (15 oz. size)
1 small can tomato paste (optional)
1 T. oregano
3 T. granulated garlic
½ -1 t. crushed red pepper depending on how hot you like it
1 T. chili powder
Salt and pepper to taste
2 cans red chili beans
2 cans red kidney beans
In a large soup pan brown meat and onion, add spices and brown for another 5-10 minutes. Add canned tomatoes, sauce and paste. Rinse out each can using about ¼ of a can of water and pour that into soup.

Add both kinds of beans at this point.

Simmer for 2-3 hours. This chili only gets better every day, so don't be afraid to make it a couple of days in advance of serving it. The water will evaporate as it is cooking. Be sure to stir occasionally and be careful not to burn.
This chili can be done in a crock-pot and simmered all day long. If using a crock-pot, brown meat, onion and spices in a skillet. Place meat mixture in crock-pot and add all other ingredients, but do not add as much water.

When our son, Josh, and my nephew, Eddie Harris, sponsored the first Harris-Furci Chili Cook Off, I brought this recipe. Not sure why it didn't win, but it sure was funny that my chili was the only one totally gobbled up!

Cream of Cauliflower Soup

In a soup pot:
Sauté 2 T. olive oil
2 T. butter
2 leeks, including 2 inches of greens, chopped
1 celery rib, chopped
Cook for 10 minutes
Add 2 T. finely minced garlic for the last 5 minutes
Stir in:
2 t. ginger, 2 t. curry and cook for 1 min
Add 6 cups chicken broth, juice of ½ lemon
1 head of cauliflower, cut into small pieces
Bring to boil…reduce to simmer until cauliflower is tender approximately 15 minutes.
Cool then puree, until smooth then add 1 cup of half & half
Add more broth if necessary and salt and pepper to taste.

Steph's Chicken Tortilla Soup
Great game day soup!

In a soup pot combine:
½ cup chopped onion
3 boneless chicken breasts, cooked and cubed
1 clove garlic
¼ t. chili powder
¼ t. ground cumin
2 cans chicken broth (14 oz.)
1 can diced tomatoes (14 oz.)
1 can green chilies (4 oz.)
4 T. cilantro
½ cup shredded cheddar cheese
1 or 2 cans white beans. Top with crisp chips when serving.

Irene's Lemon Soup

You'll think you're in Athens Greece when you taste this!

Ingredients:
40 ounces of chicken broth
½ cup long grain rice
2 eggs
3 T. fresh lemon juice
1 t. grated lemon zest
Sea salt and freshly ground white pepper to taste
2 T. chopped dill or parsley (optional)

In a large saucepan, bring chicken broth to a boil. Add rice, cover, reduce heat and simmer for 10 minutes or until rice is el dente'. Do not drain, set aside.
In a bowl, beat eggs until thick. Whisk in lemon juice and zest. Gradually add ½ cup hot broth from saucepan, whisking constantly. Add broth in ½ cup measures until all broth is added, whisking after each addition.
Pour mixture back into saucepan and reheat, stirring with a wooden spoon, until egg yolks and soup slightly thickens. Do not boil, or eggs will curdle. Add salt and pepper to taste. Sprinkle with dill or parsley (optional).
Serve hot or cold

The most precious things you will have around your neck are the tiny arms of your grandchild.~ Mel Burt

Veggie Soup

1 lb. browned cubed stew beef in small amount oil
Add ½ head cabbage (cut up)
Add 2 cans diced tomatoes
1 t. salt and pepper, (crushed red pepper to taste, optional)
2 t. beef bullion
Shake of Tabasco (to taste)
Cover mixture with water and begin to cook for 2-3 hours.
After 1 hour add any hard veggies i.e. carrots, parsnips,
turnips. After 2 hours, add frozen green beans, corn, and
peas. Continue simmering until well heated.

Gazpacho Soup

In a food processor, combine half of the following veggies:
*1 Onion, 1 red pepper, 1 cucumber, 2 tomatoes
Pour in a large bowl then add
V-8 juice plus Tomato juice—equal parts (12 oz.)
½ cup olive oil
½ cup red wine vinegar
1 ½ t. salt
½ t. pepper
2-3 cloves garlic crushed
¼ t. Tabasco
For guests, serve the second half of chopped veggies in
small bowls alongside the soup presentation for guests to
add to individual soup servings. Good with dollop of sour
cream and croutons.

*Optional: You can blend all of the veggies at one time.
Chill and store remaining soup in the Tomato Juice bottles.

*A favorite summer soup served chilled. Keeps in the
refrigerator for quite a few days.*

Papa's Favorite Soup
A nice variation of Italian Wedding Soup

In a stockpot make either chicken broth by boiling chicken or use canned chicken stock. Add 1 T. chicken granules. Cut up the boiled chicken into cubes or you can use 1 can of premium chicken breasts (13 oz) and add to broth.
Add:
 2 heads of escarole greens, chopped
½ cup fresh parsley (chopped)
2 bay leafs (remove before serving soup)
1 t. granulated garlic, salt and pepper to taste
½ t crushed red pepper (optional)

Boil water separately and cook ¾ cup pastina or soup pasta (drained) and add to soup.

*Optional: throw in small pre-cooked meatballs, if available….

Cook soup for about 1 hour, until the greens are wilted. In a separate saucepan, ladle out only the amount you are going to eat for that meal. Store extra soup for another day.

In a small bowl mix an egg or two (depending on the amount you're serving) and beat the egg with about 1/3 cup of grated Parmesan cheese, per egg. Drop into HOT soup so the egg mixture cooks thoroughly and then serve.

*Most Italian meat markets sell a meatball mixture of veal, pork and beef with seasonings that I buy for quick almost homemade meatballs.

This soup got its name from our granddaughter Lucia. She could barely talk when she first tasted my combo soup made of Italian Wedding and Stracciatella soups. The following days all she wanted to eat was "Papa's Soup!"

John Furci's Chicken Soup

Cook 1 large package of chicken thighs in 3 quarts water
(about 12 thighs with skin)
Add: 4 cubes chicken bullion
4-5 carrots (chopped)
4 T. parsley
2 celery stalks chopped (center preferred)
½ cup coarsely chopped onion
1 can tomatoes (10 oz. size)
Add all ingredients to large stock pan. Cook until chicken
is done, remove skin and de-bone. Return to soup and add
one cup of dried pasta, such as pastina or stars and bring to
boil until pasta is cooked before serving.

Jimmie's Taco Soup
So quick and easy and so good!

Combine:
1 can fat free refried beans (16 oz.)
1 can chicken broth (14 oz.)
1 can chunk chicken (5 oz.)
1 can black beans (15 oz.)
½ cup chunky salsa *--I use medium or hot*
Mix all ingredients in pot and bring to boil. Simmer for 10
minutes, stirring constantly. Serve with cheese and chips

*I often make soups to enjoy for days. Enjoy these delicious
soups with fresh baked crusty bread from your neighbor-
hood bakery.*

Pumpkin Soup

Sauté 1 large onion with ¼ cup butter until limp
Add ½ t. curry powder and sauté for 2 minutes
Use food processor to blend onions, and 1-2 boneless
chicken breasts, cooked and cubed.
Place in large soup pot and add:
2 cups canned pumpkin, 1 ½ t. salt
2 ½ cups chicken stock
Simmer for 45 minutes
When ready to serve, add 2 cups heavy cream (optional)
and cook until hot. Garnish with sour cream, cinnamon or
parsley. *When counting calories I leave out the cream.*

*One memorable Thanksgiving, our dear friends, the
Shrodes, served this pumpkin soup in small, carved out
pumpkins. It was an elegant and creative beginning to the
feast that we have been so fortunate to share during the
many years of our friendship with Fred and Mary Ellen.
Bless you both for always encouraging me in the culinary
arts!*

Broccoli Mushroom Soup

1 lb. fresh broccoli cleaned and cut into small pieces
Steam in ½ cup water until tender, do not drain. Set aside
8 ounces fresh mushrooms washed and sliced
Heat 8 ounces of butter in a saucepan over medium heat
Add ½ to ¾ cup flour to make a roux, cook for 2-4 minutes
Add 1 quart chicken stock stirring with a wire whisk and
bring to a boil. Turn heat to low
Add broccoli, mushrooms, 1 Quart of Half and Half
1 t. salt, ¼ t. pepper, and ¼ t. crushed tarragon.
Heat but do not boil

*Sometimes for fun I add different types of mushrooms along
with regular mushrooms.*

Chicken, Broccoli and Black Bean Soup

I have included several "secret" recipes from chefs during our travels. Most restaurant owners love to reveal a good recipe! This "George's at the Cove" is one such good one!

Sauté:
¼ cup unsalted butter, ½ cup diced carrots, ½ cup diced onions, ½ cup diced celery
1 cup broccoli stems, peeled, diced, (sauté 5 minutes)
Add:
2 t. thyme
1 t. sweet dried basil
2 t. oregano
Sauté for 5 minutes more
Add:
¼ cup white wine and deglaze the pan
Add:
4 cups chicken broth and reduce by ⅓
Add:
1 T. Worcestershire sauce
½ t. Tabasco
Add:
*1 cup smoked chicken chunks *(grilled chicken will do)*
1 cup canned black beans
1 cup broccoli florets
Simmer for 5 minutes
Add:
2 cups of heavy cream, simmer for 5 minutes more and season with salt and pepper to taste
2 T. cornstarch (with water) can be used to thicken if needed.
Add ¼ cup butter in soup piece by piece, stirring constantly
*Smoked Chicken: On a covered grill smoke boneless chicken cooking to medium rare. Use apple wood chips in grill.

Lena's Asparagus Soup

3 pounds fresh asparagus, rinsed
8 cups chicken stock
4 T. butter
1 cup shallots, minced
1 cup leeks, whites only, well rinsed
1 T. minced garlic
½ t. ground white pepper
1 T. chopped fresh tarragon or chervil
1 T. of flour
Greek yogurt
Red pepper

Trim top tips from the asparagus, for the garnish. Cut the remaining tender stalks in to ½ inch pieces (reserve). In a medium pot bring the stock to a boil. Add woody stems, lower the heat and simmer to infuse the flavor for 20-30 minutes. Remove stems and discard. Reserving stock, add decorative tips to stock and blanch for 1-2 minutes. Remove and put into ice water. Drain on paper towel and reserve for garnish. In a medium stock pan melt the butter, add shallots and leeks and cook until tender about 3 minutes. Add garlic for 1 min. Add chopped asparagus stalks, salt, pepper and cook stirring for 2 minutes. Add 1 T. flour and mix, red pepper to taste. Add broth tarragon and simmer until asparagus are very tender 15-20 minutes. Remove from heat. Purée soup in blender until smooth. Adjust seasoning to taste.

If serving right away, return to medium heat and add the cream and tips. Cook, stirring until the soup is warmed thoroughly, about 3 minutes.

Notes

Salads
&
Special Dressings

Notes

Susan's Italian Salad Dressing

I probably receive more compliments on this dressing than any other. I swear by it! However, do not substitute any of these ingredients because it sure won't be as good!

1 package Good Seasons Italian or Zesty Italian Dressing
½ cup good olive oil
¼ cup *red wine* vinegar
1 large clove crushed garlic
Use NO water

Super Salad

Use quantities of your choice, the flavors are a nice mix.

Toss large bowl of your favorite lettuce with the following:
Mandarin oranges
Sunflower seeds
Raisins
Tomatoes
Red onions
Monterey Jack cheese
Pepper chicken
Serve with sweet and sour dressing.

Cauliflower Salad

1 large head of Cauliflower broken into small pieces
1 medium onion (chopped)
1 bag shredded Parmesan cheese (8 ounces)
1 pound bacon cut up and fried until crispy
Mix: Equal parts of sour cream and mayonnaise ¾ to 1 cup.
Combine all ingredients with dressing
½ cup frozen peas (thawed) can be added.
Make ahead...it keeps for days.

Fred's Cesar Salad Dressing

2 to 2 ½ cups olive oil
1 cup shredded Parmesan cheese (8 oz.)
3 ounces of hard Parmesan cheese, grated
Scant ¼ cup champagne vinegar
2 heaping tablespoons of mayonnaise
6 large cloves of garlic (minced or pressed)
½ tube anchovy paste
2 shakes Worcestershire sauce
Juice from 1 ½ lemons
All measurements are approximate…

Wonderful Salad

1 head romaine lettuce
1 cup sliced celery
½ to ¾ cup red onion, chopped
1 can mandarin oranges (drained)

Sauté:
2 T. Butter
½ cup slivered almonds
2 T. Brown Sugar
(Set aside)
If you make extra, zip lock and save for future use.

Dressing: ¼ cup oil, ¼ cup tarragon vinegar,
2 T. sugar, 1 t. parsley, pinch of red pepper,
¼ t. pepper, ½ t. salt.
Top salad with almonds just before serving.

Fabulous Strawberry Salad Ala Molly

1 head of Romaine lettuce cut in 1-inch pieces
1 head of Boston lettuce, torn in bite-size pieces
½ cup walnuts, chopped
1 pint fresh strawberries, sliced
1 cup shredded Monterey Jack cheese (can use Mozzarella)

Dressing:
1 cup veggie oil
½ t. paprika
½ cup red wine vinegar
½ t. salt and ¼ t. pepper
¾ cup sugar
2 cloves minced or pressed garlic
(I make this dressing to have on hand to whip up this salad quickly during the summer months)

Dr. Tanner's wife, Molly, introduced this salad as a beautiful and tasty addition to any summer meal. I always get raves about it when served to company. The first time I served Daryl and Barbara this salad, she ate two more helpings instead of dessert!

Watermelon and Feta Salad
The sweet and salty combination is fabulous on the taste buds! Add salted sunflower seeds for a nice crunch.

Arugula and spring mix greens (5 cups)
1 cup diced watermelon (melon must be tiny cubes not chunks)
½ cup crumbled feta cheese
2 or 3 T.'s Susan's salad dressing (see page 47)
Mix and serve!

When one has tasted watermelon he knows what the angels eat. ~ Mark Twain

Biltmore Chicken Pasta Salad

4-6 Chicken Breasts…cooked, cooled and cut in bite size pieces. *Don't overcook. Sometimes I do this a day ahead, bag it, refrigerate and then use when ready. Just to save time. See poached chicken recipe on page 73.*
Boil:
1 lb. tri-colored spiral pasta ala dente …rinse with cool water and drain
Combine:
2 bunches of green onions, (include the green stems when chopping up) …*I usually cut down the onion to about 6-8 inches, then cut into small pieces*
1 large red pepper diced (optional)
2 handfuls of fresh bean sprouts (rinsed and dried)
2 cans of sliced water chestnuts (rinsed and drained)

Combine:
2 cups mayonnaise
½ t. ginger
½ cup soy sauce
½ t. ground pepper
Mix dressing into pasta and chill before serving. (Best made a day before serving).

This salad was a favorite of our son, Josh, during college. In fact, his college buddies still remember it and request it whenever in town visiting him and his wife, Lena!

Simple Salad Dressing

¼ cup each red wine and cider vinegar, ½ t. salt, ¼ t. pepper, 1 clove crushed garlic, 1 cup oil, pinch of parsley and dry or wet mustard to taste. Shake together and store in refrigerator.

Mexican Chopped Salad with Honey-Lime Dressing

Ingredients:
1 can black beans, rinsed and well drained
1 can corn
¾ cup peeled and chopped jicama (Mexican potato)
¾ cup thinly sliced radishes (optional)
1 ripe avocado, diced
1 red bell pepper, chopped
¼ cup crumbled reduced-fat feta cheese
¾ cup chopped tomato
Combine ingredients ahead of time and add tomatoes just before serving

Honey-Lime Dressing:
½ cup olive oil
½ cup fresh lime juice
1 t. prepared mustard
1 t. dry mustard
1 t. apple cider vinegar
2 T. honey
2 T. Cilantro
1 clove crushed garlic
1 t. chopped jalapeno pepper
Dash of crushed red pepper, salt and pepper to taste

Combine above ingredients pour over veggie mixture. Can be served over chopped romaine lettuce. This will stay in refrigerator for several days.

When I first tasted this it was as an appetizer at a friend's home. I could have cared less about the rest of the dinner, I loved it so much. Debbie is a recipe tweaker also, so she gets full credit for this wonderful salad/salsa. Thanks Debbie!

Angie's Chinese Cabbage Salad

The first time Angie made this for us, I skipped the filet mignon and ate this as my entire meal!

Combine: 1 Large Head of Napa Cabbage cut into bite-size pieces
1 bunch long-stemmed green onions (use whole onion) chopped, set aside.
The original recipe calls for doing this a day ahead of time, however I sometimes do it the day I will serve it.

Sauté:
½ stick of butter
2 packages uncooked noodles from Ramen Noodle Soup (crushed) Use one packet of seasoning with noodles and one in dressing.
4 oz. slivered almonds
Add 1 oz. sesame seeds last…so not to burn

Dressing:
½ cup apple cider vinegar
1 t. soy sauce
½ cup canola oil
½ cup sugar (can use ½ Splenda and ½ sugar)
Seasoning packet from the Ramen Noodles
Dressing can be kept in refrigerate for weeks.

Some recipes I have seen put both packs of seasoning in the dressing…I don't think it matters. This salad makes a meal! But can also be served with grilled chicken on top.

Dining with one's friends and beloved family is certainly one of life's primal and most innocent delights, one that is both soul satisfying and eternal. ~ Julia Child

Barbara's Fabulous Pasta Salad

This versatile salad is featured on every buffet of mine!

1 16 oz. bow tie pasta, cooked el dente, rinse, set aside

In a large bowl combine:
⅓ cup olive oil
2 regular size cans of Del Monte brand tomatoes with basil and oregano
2-3 cloves of garlic finely chopped or pressed
1 cup chopped red onion
1 can sliced black olives
¼ cup minced fresh parsley
Salt and pepper to taste
4-5 leaves fresh basil, finely chopped
Add cooled pasta
6-8 ounces of crumbled feta cheese – toss together.

This dish is best made a day or two ahead of time. It gets better every day! Just stir every so often. Keep refrigerated until serving. Some people prefer serving at room temperature.

Broccoli Delight Salad

3 bunches of broccoli cut into flowerets
½ cup raisins
¼ to ½ lb of fried bacon (crumbled)

Dressing:
¼ cup chopped onion
2 T. sugar
3 T. apple cider vinegar

Pour dressing over broccoli mixture right before serving and add ½ cup pecans or sunflower seeds to top.

Spanish Orange Salad

Mix the following and let stand for 30 minutes:
¼ cup olive oil
2 T. wine vinegar
¾ t. salt
⅛ t. pepper
3 oranges, peeled and sliced thin

Pour mixture over 8 cups of torn greens, ½ cup black olives, sliced. Top with ¼ cup of sunflower seeds.

Karen's Mennonite Potato Salad
My son-in-law Josh especially loves this authentic dish.

Mix together and set aside:
1 ½ cups mayonnaise
1 cup sugar
2 T. prepared mustard
3 T. vinegar
1 ½ t. salt
⅛ to ¼ tsp. celery seed (if omitting celery)
Dash of onion salt

Grate together:
10 medium potatoes, cooked in the skins and cooled completely before peeling
5 hard boiled eggs, peeled and chopped
Optional:
¾ cup chopped onion
¾ cup celery
Gently fold dressing into the grated potatoes and eggs and cool completely before serving. Sprinkle with paprika. *The key to this recipe is grating the potatoes. A ricer can be used instead of a grater.*

Pickled Beets and Eggs

Hard cook as many eggs as you will want, peel and set aside (6 to 12)

Combine the juice from a 32 oz jar of pickled beets
My favorite brand is Safie's Home Style Sweet Pickled Beets. (I find them at Giant Eagle)

Combine:
Juice from the beets
¾ cup vinegar
¼ cup water
1 T. sugar

Optional:
Couple of cloves
Sliced Onion
Granulated Garlic
Pour this mixture over the hard cooked eggs and add beets back to container.
Hopefully the liquid covers your eggs and they will turn purple within a few (4-5) days.
Can be served on an egg dish like you serve deviled eggs, or serve them whole along with the beets.

If you are in a hurry to get the eggs to absorb the beet juice stick a straight pin in each end of the egg, making a tiny hole, they will turn purple much faster.

The discovery of a new dish does more for the happiness of mankind than the discovery of a star. ~ Anthelme Brillat-Savarin

Christmas Crunch Salad

Salad ingredients:
4 cups broccoli flowerets
4 cups cauliflower flowerets
1 red onion coarsely chopped
2 cups chopped tomato

Dressing:
1 cup mayonnaise
½ cup sour cream
1 T. vinegar
1 T. sugar
Salt and pepper to taste

Mariann's Spinach Salad

2 packages fresh spinach
½ package seasoned croutons
1 lb cooked bacon (crumbled)
Optional: fresh mushrooms, hard boiled eggs, strawberries
Dressing:
Blend in blender
6 green onions (tops and all)
⅔ cup sugar
1 t. salt
½ t. pepper
1 t. celery seed
3 t. dry mustard
When thoroughly blended
Add:
½ cup red wine vinegar
½ cup olive oil
Blend 5 minutes in blender high to med high *(very important to blend this length of time, it will separate)*

Furci's 1905 Salad

This is an entire meal...Beth's favorite!

Choose two different kinds of green lettuce. *Our favorites are Romaine, Red Romaine, Boston or simply Head Lettuce.*
Wash, tear and spin generous amounts of any two.

Chop into small pieces:
Deli Turkey
Deli Ham
Swiss cheese
Tomatoes
Onions (sweet or purple)
1 can black olives (sliced)
Green olives (sliced)
Add:
Finely Grated Parmesan Cheese
Croutons

Because all of the chopping is time consuming, I always do it ahead of time and place the above ingredients in the refrigerator. When ready to serve add the amount of each of the chopped ingredients of your choice in with the two kinds of lettuce.
Toss with Susan's Italian salad dressing! (see page 47)
Add croutons last

During our years of living in Sarasota, Florida we often visited the Columbia Restaurant on St. Armand's Circle. We always loved what they called their 1905 Salad, made tableside. Their take on it is a little different than ours, but we still lovingly call it 1905 Salad.

Notes

Meats and Fish Entrees

Notes

Yummy Tenderloin

Choose 6-7 lb. beef tenderloin
Season with garlic, either granulated or fresh (or both)
Bake at 450 degrees for 10-15 minutes—Reduce heat
Bake at 400 degrees for 45-75 minutes
Approximately 50 minutes for rare to medium-rare

Baked Italian Chicken

Slice thinly one large onion, place in large disposable tin foil baking pans
Wash and dry chicken with skin place over onions, salt generously with sea salt, can use plain.

Refrigerate overnight, if possible, sometimes I do this in the morning if am not able to do overnight. It tenderizes the meat. Many years ago I read a tip from a recipe from someone who won a "Best Fried Chicken" contest. The only difference in my recipe and the winner was the salting trick, so I adapted it to my chicken recipes.

Use lots of the following spices:
Dried oregano, dried or fresh basil, granulated garlic, onion flakes, Lawry's Seasoned salt, small amounts of finely crushed red pepper and black pepper. *Don't be afraid to use lots of spice.*
Cover baking dish tightly with foil
Bake for 2 hours at 300-325 degrees. *When you remove the foil you may want to brown the skin of the chicken lightly. Sometimes it doesn't need it.*

This is the chicken recipe featured in the story about me in "Don't Get Caught in the Act!" (Page 197)

Balsamic Herb Lamb Chops

10 baby lamb chops
⅓ cup olive oil
3 T. balsamic vinegar
2 large cloves garlic, crushed
1 T. fresh rosemary, chopped
2 T. honey
2 t. Dijon mustard
1 t. dried oregano
Salt and pepper to taste
Place lamb in a shallow dish. Salt chops, let sit for 1 hour.

Combine: olive oil, vinegar, spices in a separate bowl. Coat chops in marinade and marinate for 2 hours, turning after 1 hour. Grill for about 5 minutes for medium.

Tuna Steaks
So easy, nutritious and delicious

4 Tuna Steaks
Combine:
¼ cup soy sauce
1 T. Japanese rice wine vinegar
1 T. honey
2 T. sesame oil
Divide sauce into halves, keeping one half for dipping when fish is prepared
To the other half of the mixture, add 1 T. rice wine vinegar and coat tuna steaks
Place sesame seeds in a shallow dish and press tuna into seeds, do both sides
Heat sesame oil until very hot and place tuna into a skillet until done
The recipe suggested cooking steaks for 30 seconds, but I cook them several minutes on each side. Serve with dipping sauce and wasabi.

John's Chicken Piccata

This is a delicious and fancy recipe not difficult to prepare.

4 medium chicken breasts (rinse and pat dry)
Slice thin and pound even thinner, then lightly flour and fry
in about ¼ cup of canola oil…(add more oil as needed)
until golden brown, salt lightly.

Set aside cooked chicken

Wipe the skillet out with a paper towel and return to stove
on medium heat.
Add ½ cup lemon juice (use fresh lemon)
2 cups Chablis wine and some pieces of lemon rind

Add:
⅓ cup fresh chopped parsley,
1 clove minced garlic,
1 ½ ounces of capers and 1 t. pepper
Return chicken to skillet and cook over high heat for 5
minutes.

Add ½ stick of butter to this mixture right before ready to
serve. Slice lemon very thinly and serve chicken over rice.

*"The food at my restaurants is mostly the food of Italy's
grandmothers.* ~ Mario Batali

Beef Vegetable Stew with Dumplings

Brown 3 lbs. of beef (cut into 1 lb pieces) in 3 Tablespoons oil. Remove from pot and lightly brown cut-up veggies in meat drippings.
Veggies: 4 large carrots, 3 medium turnips, 4 large celery stalks, 1 large onion

Stir in 2 Tablespoons flour to make the soup thick and cook one minute.

Return meat to pan.

Add: 6 cups of water, 1 16oz. can of tomatoes with juice, 48 ounces of beef broth, 1 tsp. salt, ½ t. dried thyme, and ¼ t. pepper. Heat to a boil. Reduce heat to low; cover and simmer for 1 ½ to 2 hours or until meat is tender. Cut meat into bite size pieces and remove fat or bones. Return meat to soup; reheat to a boil.

Prepare dumplings: In saucepan over medium heat add ½ cup water and 4 Tablespoons margarine to boil. Remove from heat. Stir in ½ cup flour until mixture forms a ball. Beat in 2 large eggs until satiny.

Into simmering soup, drop dough by level teaspoon. Cover and simmer for 5 minutes. Add 1 box frozen spinach, (10 oz.) thawed; cook 5 more minutes until dumplings are cooked thoroughly.

This was my first introduction to turnips and I loved them. The dumplings add such a wonderful flair to an old fashion dish. I suppose you could make the recipe in a Crockpot and add the dumplings for the last hour or so.

Simple Salmon Patties

Combine:
1 can salmon (15 oz.) drain water from fish
1 beaten egg
1 small onion, minced
¾ to 1 cup crushed crackers *(I like Ritz)* use enough so the mixture is semi-firm, but pliable
Salt and pepper
Can add a little water, if mixture is too thick
Small amount crushed red pepper (optional)

Form into equal balls and then press into patties on a cutting board. Dust with flour, white or wheat. Then lift the patties onto your hand and dust the other side. Flipping from hand to hand will release extra flour.
Immediately place in warm skillet with 2-3 Tablespoons melted butter on medium heat until crispy on each side. If you cook these in batches, refresh the butter with each batch.

I have always loved this dish, much to Don's dismay! He hates even the smell of salmon. When an Aunt passed away and we were preparing for a get together after the funeral, someone mentioned their love for grandma's salmon patties. It was amazing to me how many members of our clan loved this dish. I quadrupled the recipe and there was not one left. There's nothing like a favorite dish from our past to brighten our spirits and bring back good memories!

Genuine Southern Fried Chicken

1 chicken cut up (3 ½ lbs)
3 t. salt, divided
Vegetable oil for frying
¼ cup butter
¾ cup All Purpose flour
½ t. ground pepper

*Sprinkle chicken with 2 t. salt. Place on a platter, cover with wax paper and refrigerate for 4 hours or overnight.

Pour 1-inch oil into a large, deep, heavy skillet. Add butter and heat over medium-high heat to 375 degrees.

Rinse salt off chicken under cold water.

Mix: Flour, 1 t. salt and ½ t. pepper in a paper bag, shake well. Add half the chicken and shake to coat well. Shake off excess flour. Repeat with remaining pieces of chicken.

Place chicken to skillet in a single layer so the pieces do not touch. *(If necessary, cook in batches).*

Store fried chicken in a 200 degree oven to keep warm. Fry the chicken pieces evenly until golden brown on each side, turning once, about 15 minutes total. Drain well on paper towels, serve hot. Makes 6 servings.

See my comment regarding the importance of salting in my "hints" section.

I think no matter what the occasion may be, you can never go wrong by showing up at the dinner table with a hot plate of fried chicken. ~ Paula Deen

Veal Milanese

I love to serve this veal with a garnish of arugula, onion, and tomato with Italian dressing.

Dust veal slices in flour, salt and pepper (can use plastic bag).

Dip floured veal in beaten egg and a small amount of milk.

Mix: 1 cup Italian style seasoned bread crumbs with 1 t. granulated garlic, 1 t. oregano, 1 t. basil and 2 T. Parmesan cheese. Then coat veal with the seasoned breadcrumbs.

Sauté in equal amounts of olive oil and butter on medium high heat in skillet, drain on paper towels.

Veal Piccata ala Bob Furci

In the true tradition of Italian cooking, my brother-in-law never gave me amounts—just ingredients! You're on your own when you attempt this recipe!

Combine flour, salt, pepper, and granulated garlic to bread veal in this mixture.

Fry breaded veal in hot oil, blot off on paper towels.
In same skillet, use the drippings from the veal and a little olive oil and a little flour.

Add sliced fresh mushrooms, fresh parsley, garlic salt and pepper, sauté together.
Add 1-2 cans of chicken broth and 1 cup of white wine. Return veal and simmer on low heat for 45 minutes to 1 hour.

To me, life without veal stock, pork fat, sausage, organ meat, demi-glace, or even stinky cheese is a life not worth living. ~ Anthony Bourdain, celebrity chef

Shrimp Scampi

This is a favorite to serve as an appetizer or main course.

Use equal parts butter and olive oil (½ cup), melt together
in a large saucepan
Add finely crushed red pepper (½-¼ teaspoon)
Add lots of fresh parsley (½ cup)
Add ½ cup white wine
Juice from 1 whole lemon
Use 4-6 cloves of fresh garlic, minced or pressed
1 t. salt
1 t. granulated garlic
Bring to a soft boil
Add 1 or 2 lbs. shrimp, cleaned and thawed
Cook for about 5-10 minutes. Or until shrimp turns pink
Don't overcook as shrimp will toughen
Serve w/pasta or use as an appetizer with French bread.

John Furci's Leg of Lamb

Make slits in a 5 lb. lamb and put garlic in the slits also
sprinkle with garlic powder, rosemary
(Optional) Cut up 4 large potatoes and 1 Large Onion,
place around roast
Put ½ inch of water in pan and tent with tin foil.
Preheat oven to 500 degrees and cook for 20 minutes, then
reduce to 350 degrees for remaining time. Cook for
approximately 2 hours. (20 minutes per lb.)
When meat is almost done, uncover for last 20 minutes, add
young peas, and fresh parsley. Use liquid to serve over
pasta.

There is no such thing as a little garlic! ~ Anonymous

Aunt Mary's Meatballs

1 lb. each of the following ground meats: beef, veal and
pork (3 lbs. altogether)
6 cloves of garlic minced
¾ loaf of French bread dried
Lots of fresh parsley
Salt and pepper to taste
2 eggs
1 cup Parmesan cheese

Soak bread in water to soften then break into small pieces
squeeze out excess water.

Mix in remaining ingredients *(mixture should be mushy)*
then add chopped meat. Salt again. Fry or bake in oven 375
degrees for 30-40 minutes.

*For years I faithfully made Aunt Mary's meatballs.
However, I must credit our daughter, Heidi, for
enlightening me to Carfagna's (our local Italian grocery)
meatball "ready" mix of ground beef, veal and pork. Most
Italian grocers sell a meatball mix, readymade. When I
purchase this mix I make medium and small meatballs, fry
them and freeze them for future use with pasta or soups.
Forgive me, Aunt Mary!*

*Cooking has always brought me a happiness that I didn't
think was available. I just fire up the stove, and things start
to fade away.* ~ Paula Deen

Fred's Tilapia Over Pasta

Seems more time consuming then it is. So delicious!

Ingredients:
1.5 lb. fresh Tilapia (6 to 8 filets)
Garlic (8-12 cloves)
Olive oil & butter
1 onion, chopped
½ lb. celery or 1 package of hearts of celery (chopped)
1 jar capers (4-6 oz.)
½ cup of white wine
1 cup chicken stock
¼ cup fresh parsley, chopped
Lemon juice from 1 ½ lemons
½ to 1 t. crushed red pepper *(see my helpful hints)*
Tomatoes (optional)
1 lb angel hair pasta (prepare your pan to boil pasta)

In a large skillet: sauté lightly 8-12 cloves of chopped garlic in 3 T. olive oil and 3 T. butter for 3 minutes, take garlic out of pan and set aside to use later.

Wash, pat dry and lightly dust fish fillets with flour
In same skillet, brown the fish. (About 3 minutes per side). *You may add a little more oil and butter.* Remove fish and set aside.
In the same pan, sauté chopped onion and celery, you can add a little more oil or butter if needed. Cook on medium heat about 5-8 minutes or until celery starts to soften. Add the chicken stock, white wine, parsley, garlic, lemon juice, red pepper, adding fish last. Bring to a soft boil for about 7-10 minutes.

This is about when you "throw the pasta" to cook (4-11 minutes) depending on what pasta you like—it's great over linguine, but my favorite is angel hair, which only cooks for 4 minutes.

70

Minutes before pasta is cooked, add 1 jar of capers and ½ stick of butter to fish. *I don't use salt because the capers are salty…(but if you're not going to use the capers, you might want to add salt).*

Remember this will be the juice for your pasta, so make enough for the amount of pasta you will cook. I would guess 1 cup of chicken stock, and ½ cup of white wine works well for 1lb. of pasta.

The original recipe calls for topping with chopped tomatoes. For me this is optional, I do it both ways. The original recipe was NOT served over pasta. One time we had leftovers and Don said let's do a little pasta with butter/olive oil/garlic and we loved it even more than the original – thus this dish was born!

Kathy's Chicken Wings
Easy and delicious way to whip up a quick appetizer to go!

In a plastic bag
Combine:
1 cup regular bread crumbs
1 package of taco seasoning
Shake raw chicken wing-drummettes, until well coated
Place wings on a jelly roll pan or baking sheet with sides.
Bake at 400 degrees for 30 minutes, turning once during baking process.

Grilled Shrimp with Orzo
From my Ohio neighbor Sharon Oda

8 ounces orzo (about 1 ⅓ cups) ·
6 ½ T. extra-virgin olive oil, divided
4 T. red wine vinegar, divided
2 medium zucchini or summer squash (9 ounces total)
Cut zucchini lengthwise into ¼ inch-thick slices
1 red or yellow bell pepper, quartered
3 T. purchased pesto
2 T. fresh limejuice
1 pound uncooked large shrimp, peeled, de-veined
2 cups tomatoes, fresh cut in cubes
½ cup thinly sliced fresh basil leaves (*save a few sprigs for garnish)*
1 ball fresh mozzarella cheese, (8-ounce) cut into ½ inch cubes

Preparation:
Cook orzo. Drain. Rinse with cold water; drain. Transfer to large bowl and toss with 1 T. oil. Set aside.

Over medium heat:
Whisk 2 T. oil and 2 T. vinegar in small bowl. Brush zucchini and bell pepper with hot oil mixture, and then sprinkle with salt and pepper.

Whisk: pesto, lime juice, remaining 3 ½ T. oil, and remaining 2 T. vinegar in small bowl for pesto vinaigrette.

Place shrimp in medium bowl. Add 2 T. pesto vinaigrette; toss to coat.

Grill: zucchini and bell pepper until crisp tender, about 3 minutes per side for zucchini and 4 minutes per side for bell pepper. Transfer to work surface.

Sprinkle shrimp with salt and pepper; grill until charred and cooked through, 2 to 3 minutes per side. Place shrimp in bowl with prepared orzo.

Chop: zucchini and bell pepper; add to bowl with orzo. Add remaining vinaigrette, tomatoes, sliced basil, and mozzarella; toss to combine. Season to taste with salt and pepper. *(This dish can be done ahead and chilled)*. Garnish with basil sprigs to serve cold or at room temperature.

Chinese Poached Chicken

1 whole chicken (2-3 pounds) or chicken breasts with skin

Bring 3 quarts of water to boil in a deep pot. Submerge the chicken and boil over high heat for 12 minutes, keeping the lid in place.

Turn heat off and allow the chicken to cool down in the broth for about 2 hours. Leave lid in place. The remaining broth can be frozen for soup chicken stock.

I found this is the best way to prepare moist chicken for use in salads or casseroles.

Years ago, this method was taught at a Chinese cooking class we participated in with several couples. Our Chinese instructor declared: "You Americans cook chicken way too long!"

Notes

Sauces & Marinades

Notes

Furci Family Red Sauce

This is a large amount, but leftover sauce is always used around here. You can cut this recipe in half.

In Large sauce pan fry:
4-5 pieces of sausage mild or hot (preferred)
Pieces of fresh pork…neck bones, ribs, short ribs
After browning add:
1 large chopped onion with 6 or 7 cloves of chopped garlic and sauté for 5-10 minutes
Add:
Fresh 6-8 leaves of fresh basil, ¾ cup fresh parsley, 1 ½ T. of oregano, 2 T. granulated garlic, 1 t. finely crushed red pepper, salt and pepper
(Can use dried spices when fresh aren't available)
Don't be afraid to use lots of spice.
Brown spices

Add:
2 large cans of crushed tomatoes
2 medium cans of tomato sauce
1 can tomato paste (optional) *Don adds this, but I don't.*
Rinse cans with water and add water to sauce (about ¼ of each can)
As the sauce thickens, the water will cook off.
Add ½-¾ cup wine
Cover and cook for several hours (2-4 hours) uncover and continue to simmer on low heat for another hour. *The sauce can sit for hours before serving.*

Throw in cooked meatballs for a yummy spaghetti dinner!
See Aunt Mary for meatball recipe, page 69.

Best Chicken Marinade

I use boneless skinless chicken, I like tenderloins or breast. If I want to use chicken with skin (which does keep the meat moist) I debone it. If you go to a butcher, they will debone it for you. Chicken with bone takes much longer to cook, especially when grilling, so it has a tendency to dry out. Pour a generous amount of Italian salad dressing (see Susan's Italian salad dressing (page 47) to cover the bottom of a flat dish.

Sprinkle chicken with:
Granulated garlic
Lawry's seasoned salt
Oregano
Parsley
Crushed red pepper
Turn the chicken over after 30 minutes before grilling. The larger the piece of chicken the longer you need to marinate it.

Variations:
Add a little soy sauce or teriyaki to the salad dressing for an oriental flavor
Add a little Worcestershire for a bolder taste
Add honey if you want a nice glaze
Grill to your liking!

Tenderloin Steak Marinade
We love this marinade for filet mignon

¼ cup olive oil
¼ cup red wine vinegar
¼ t. salt and ¼ t pepper
Pinch of crushed red pepper
2 T. Teriyaki sauce

2 T. Worcestershire sauce
3 leaves of fresh basil (chopped)
1 t. oregano
1 t. granulated garlic
1 large clove of garlic (crushed)
Combine ingredients and place steaks in for 1 hour before grilling.

Misty Mango Salsa
Best served over baked fish

Combine:
2 Celestial Misty Mango tea bags
½ cup white vinegar (let stand 20 minutes)

In a bowl combine:
2 ripe mangos, peeled and diced
½ red bell pepper (chopped)
4 fresh chives, snipped into small bits
Add ¼ cup of the tea mix and toss to combine.
Brush fish *(Swordfish is our favorite)* with remaining tea and grill until done. Top with salsa. Serve with rice.

Doc's Flank Steak Marinade

½ cup teriyaki
¼ cup soy sauce
3 cloves fresh garlic, 5 leaves of fresh basil, ¼ cup fresh parsley
3 T. olive oil and 3 T. red wine vinegar
1 T. oregano
½ t. granulated garlic
Dash of salt and pepper

Place flank steaks in a shallow dish and pour marinade over it to let stand for 1 hour (turning after 30 minutes). Grill to your preference. Slice on angle.

Marinade for Pork Tenderloin

Trim fat, place meat in a flat bowl
Rub roast with paper towel soaked in vinegar
Make Rub:
1 T. dry mustard, salt and pepper
1-2 T. olive oil, 2 t. soy sauce
3 cloves finely chopped garlic
1 t. finely chopped rosemary, 1 t. Cajun spice
Mix with fingers into paste, apply to meat and leave on for
1 hour to all day. Sear both sides at high on grill, reduce
heat to low, turn constantly. Cook for 20-25 minutes.

Fig Sauce
For Pork Loin

Fig Sauce:
2 ½ cups Port wine
1 ¼ cup chicken broth
8 Mission Figs, chopped
2 sprigs fresh rosemary
2 cinnamon sticks
1 T. honey
1 T. unsalted butter
¼ t. salt
¼ t. freshly ground pepper

Combine first 6 ingredients. Simmer for 30 minutes until
sauce reduces in half. Discard the rosemary and cinnamon
sticks. Transfer mixture to blender and add butter, salt and
pepper. Blend until smooth. Cover and refrigerate.
Re-warm before serving over medium heat.

Preheat oven to 425 degrees.
Prepare Rub:
2 T. olive oil, 2 T. chopped fresh rosemary, 1 T. salt, and
1 ½ t. fresh ground pepper. Pour 1 cup chicken broth into

roasting pan.

Add 1 boneless pork loin (4 to 4.5 lbs)
Rub loin with prepared rub.
Place into oven…turn and baste loin every 15 minutes for
about 45 minutes longer.
When finished cooking, slice and pour remaining juices
over loin from baking dish. Serve with fig sauce on the
side.

Josh's Barbeque Chicken Marinade

Seasoning rub: Lawry's Season Salt, sea salt, granulated
garlic, Weber Grill Creation Sweet and Tangy, ground
black pepper
Combine all ingredients and rub chicken allowing it to
marinate for at least 1 hour.
Grill using: KC Masterpiece Hickory Brown Sugar Sauce

Josh's Ginger Chicken

Chicken pieces of your choice
Combine dry ingredients:
1 t. Lawry's season salt
1 t. granulated garlic
1 t. oregano, basil, dried parsley, cracked black pepper,
Essence of Emeril, Creole seasoning, Weber Grill Kickin
Chicken seasoning
Mix with:
½ cup Ken's Asian Sesame with Ginger and Soy dressing
½ cup Teriyaki Sauce
Marinate at least one hour or overnight in refrigerator. Do
not use the remaining marinade on cooked chicken. Discard
after use.

81

Notes

Pasta & That's Italian!

Notes

John's Pasta Pomodora

Don's favorite…I think my husband could eat it every night of the week!

In a large sauce pan combine 2 large and 1 small cans of Hunts diced peeled tomatoes or fresh peeled plum tomatoes

Add:
2 large cloves of minced garlic, some basil, salt and pepper, simmer for 30 minutes
In another large skillet sauté:
4 cloves minced garlic
3 T. olive oil
Add 1 medium onion julienne cut
Add 8 oz. prosciutto, thinly sliced
Sauté until golden brown
Add: ½ cup dry white wine…Chablis, not sweet wine
Add tomatoes to meat mixture
Add 2 T. chopped fresh basil
3 bay leaves (remove before serving)
Salt, pepper, red pepper to taste
Cook together for 30-45 minutes
Pour over al dente cooked pasta

Baked Pasta

I always add a little red pepper to this dish, it's just a nice variation of pasta.

Sauté 1 cup chopped onions in butter and place onions in a casserole dish
Cook pasta of your choice, spaghetti, rigatoni, or penne
Toss with red sauce (meat or marinara)
Cover onions with pasta
Generously layer mozzarella cheese on top of pasta
Optional: Sprinkle with Parmesan cheese
Bake at 350 degrees until thoroughly heated and cheese is bubbly.

Hot Peppers Italian Style

Wash and cut into halves:
12 assorted hot banana peppers
12 Jalapeno peppers
2 Habanera peppers (if you want REAL heat!) Remove most of the seeds (the more seeds, the more heat).
You can also add: red, orange, yellow or green peppers
These peppers have no heat, but add flavor and color to the dish. Set aside.

In a large skillet sauté 5 large cloves of garlic in 4 T. olive oil
Add ½ cup chopped onion, sauté for approximately 3-5 minutes
Add the peppers to skillet
Salt and pepper to taste
Cover and steam for 30-45 minutes or until peppers are soft.
When cooled place in a glass jar, cover with olive oil and store in refrigerator.

Don eats these peppers on sandwiches, steak, sausage and any dish! I suspect he may even put them on his cereal when I'm not looking. Probably the reason he has less wrinkles than me…the olive oil!

White Clam Sauce ala Susan
For Linguini

½ cup olive oil
½ cup butter
2-3 large cloves minced garlic
1 can Progresso white clam sauce
1 can minced baby clams
1 t. oregano
1 t. salt

½ t. pepper
1 T. dried parsley
½ t. dried basil
¼ t. red pepper

Melt butter and olive oil in medium size pan. Add minced garlic and spices. After garlic is lightly browned, add both cans of clams with broth. Cook over medium heat, no longer than a few minutes, cooking any longer will toughen the clams. Serve over cooked pasta.

This is one of my most difficult dishes to prepare because I'm allergic to shellfish — but it is one of my husband's favorites!

Creamy Sausage-Zucchini Sauce for Ziti

Fry: ½ lb. sweet Italian sausage browned in oil (drained) can also use spicy hot if preferred.

Using the same pan and some of the juice from sausage, sauté 1 lb. zucchini (2 large) cut into 3x1½ inch sticks, approximately 3 minutes or until tender. Drain on paper towels.
Add: 1 T. flour into drippings, stir until smooth.
Gradually stir in 1 cup of milk, cook until thickened.
Stir in ¼ cup Parmesan cheese, 1 t. basil, and salt and pepper to taste. Optional: (crushed red pepper).

Return sausage and zucchini to sauce, cooking until hot and pour over prepared Ziti pasta (12 ounces). Serve immediately.

Pasta Con Fagioli
Given to me by a famous NYC restaurateur

Ingredients:
3-4 T. olive oil
I medium onion, finely chopped
3 cloves garlic minced
¼ lb. prosciutto cut into small pieces
Sauté until golden in color

Add:
1 quart of chicken stock
1 15 oz. red kidney beans…can use garbanzo beans
1 15oz. white cannelloni beans. *I think the white beans dissolve if you put them in at this point. I have started holding them out until the pasta is almost done.*
2 bay leafs
2 T. fresh basil
Optional- 2 small potatoes, finely chopped
Cook 12-20 minutes on low heat
You can enhance the flavor by tossing a small piece of Parmesan cheese rind into the sauce for this cooking time before adding the pasta.

Add 1½ cups dry pasta and continue cooking for the recommended pasta preparation time. *I love using cavatappi noodles for this dish, because they are so fun!*
Remove bay leaves
Serve

This Italian chili can be served as a meal accompanied by a salad. Turn it into a delicious soup by adding more broth. All my grand kids love this dish. Always a crowd pleaser, too!

Everything you see I owe to spaghetti. ~ Sophia Loren, actress

Fettuccine Alfredo Sauce

Best served over fettuccine, but use any heavy pasta such as penne, rigatoni or ziti.

Heat:
1 ½ cups whole milk
1 ½ cups heavy cream
Stirring constantly until it simmers. Turn off heat.

Slowly whip in:
½ cup imported Parmesan cheese, grated
½ cup imported Romano cheese, grated
Then remove from heat.

Separate:
6 jumbo eggs (discard whites)

Beat egg yolks in a separate bowl and slowly whip a portion of the hot milk and cheese mixture (several tablespoons) to prevent eggs from cooking when added to hot sauce.
Slowly add egg yolk mixture back into the remaining cream mixture. Return to heat and stir constantly until the mixture thickens to desired consistency. *Season to taste...I added red pepper...don't salt as the cheese is salty.*

I've heard it said that Fettucini Alfredo is Macaroni and Cheese for adults. ~ Susan Furci

One of the very nicest things about life is the way we must regularly stop whatever it is we are doing and devote our attention to eating. ~ Luciano Pavarotti

Sun-Dried Tomato Chicken Pasta

1 T. olive oil
3-4 garlic cloves, minced
1 cup chopped drained sun-dried tomatoes packed in oil
1 cup heavy cream
1 6-7 oz. jar of roasted red peppers, drained and chopped
1-2 cups sliced red onion (optional)
½ t. dried crushed red pepper
1 cup chopped fresh basil leaves
1 chicken breast, cooked and cubed
2 T. Mascarpone cheese (optional)
1 cube chicken bouillon

Heat oil in skillet. Add garlic and onion: sauté 1 minute. Dissolve a chicken bouillon with 2 T. water, and add to sauté 3 more minutes. Add tomatoes, cream, red peppers, crushed pepper, and chicken. Heat 2-5 minutes. Add Mascarpone. Heat until cheese is melted. Stir in basil and simmer 1 more min.

Add 2 cups cooked penne pasta and 1 cup grated Parmesan cheese.

Spicy Peanut Noodles
Cold pasta dish

8 oz. cooked linguine or fettuccine
¼ cup vegetable oil
3 T. sesame oil
½ t. crushed red pepper
3 T. honey
2 T. soy sauce
1 t. salt
2 T. chopped fresh cilantro or parsley
¼ cup peanuts
¼ cup green onion

Heat oils and red pepper for 2 minutes. Remove from heat add honey, soy, and salt. Combine with cooked pasta. Cover and chill 4 hours or overnight. When ready to serve toss with parsley, peanuts, and onion.

Capellini with Spinach, Basil and Pine Nuts

Ingredients:
¾ to 1 cup fresh basil chopped
1 package (16 oz) Capellini (thin spaghetti)
1 cup pine nuts
¾ cup olive oil (divided, as directed in instructions)
5 large garlic cloves, minced
¾ t. dried red pepper flakes to taste
12 to 16 oz washed and trimmed spinach leaves, coarsely chopped
¾ cup grated fresh Parmesan cheese
Salt & pepper to taste

Cook pasta according to package directions.

In a wok or large skillet pan, sauté pine nuts until golden. Remove from pan and set aside.

In the same pan, heat ½ cup olive oil and sauté minced garlic and red pepper flakes for one minute.
Stir in spinach and toss over high heat until wilted, 2 to 3 minutes. Do not overcook or spinach will stick together. Drain pasta and put into a large bowl. Add remaining ¼ cup olive oil, spinach mixture, Parmesan cheese, and pine nuts. Salt and pepper to taste. Serve immediately.

The ear tests words as the palate tastes food. ~
Job 34:3

Crepes for Manicotti
Makes about 36

1 ½ cups flour
⅛ t. salt
3 eggs
1 ½ cups milk
2 T. oil or melted butter

With an electric mixer, beat eggs and sugar together before gradually adding flour and milk. Beat until mixture is smooth. Add melted butter. Set aside for not more than six hours at room temperature. When ready to cook, batter should be as thin as heavy cream. Add a little milk, if too thick.
Lightly oil a small, round frying pan skillet, heat pan to medium heat. (Six-inch skillet) Pour about ⅛ cup of batter into hot surface, using your wrist to spread batter evenly around the round surface. Cook only for a few seconds, or until edges begin to curl and crepe is golden brown. Place each crepe on a wire rack to cool, and then place wax paper between crepes to store in refrigerator or freezer.

Manicotti Filling

Mix the following: 2 lbs. ricotta with 1 cup grated Parmesan cheese, 1 cup Mozzarella cheese, 1 T. chopped fresh parsley, 2 eggs with salt and pepper to taste.
1 t. granulated garlic and a small amount of crushed red pepper.
Cover bottom of baking dish with red sauce.
If using the above crepes, spoon 2 to 3 tablespoons of filling in a line across the crepe before rolling to resemble an open-ended tube. Place seam-side down in baking dish. Cover with additional red sauce. Sprinkle with Mozzarella cheese. Bake at 325 degrees until bubbly. When using store

bought manicotti tubes found at your local grocery, follow the package directions for preparation.

Fried Spaghetti
Great way to use leftovers!

In an omelet type non-stick skillet melt 2-3 T. of butter over medium heat.
Place 2-3 cloves of garlic, thinly sliced, in skillet.
Place spaghetti on top of garlic (this is leftover thin spaghetti with red sauce)
This should be a thin layer...no more than 2 inches thick or it won't heat properly.
Do not stir at anytime while cooking this dish!
Cover with a lid so pasta is heated all the way through. Best guess on time is about 8-10 minutes depending on the heat.

Cook over medium high heat until you think pasta is golden brown and garlic is toasted to perfection.
It may take a couple of tries before you get the timing perfected...but trust me it's so good!

Turn out of the skillet much like an omelet or frittata. *I remove the lid, then place a large plate on the skillet, like a lid, while holding it securing with my left hand, I turn the skillet upside down with my right hand. I always do this over a sink, just in case. The crispy garlic should be on the top of your dish. So far I've never lost it, but please be careful if you try this! Serve with crushed red pepper and Parmesan cheese. Now that's Italian!*

This is a favorite and very good use of leftovers. Whenever we have spaghetti with red sauce, there are always leftovers. This is why!

Mushroom Risotto

Ingredients:

6 cups chicken broth, divided
3 T. olive oil, divided
1 pound Portobello mushrooms, thinly sliced
1 pound white mushrooms, thinly sliced
2 shallots, diced
1 ½ cups Arborio rice
½ cup dry white wine (Chablis)
Sea salt to taste and freshly ground black pepper to taste
3 T. finely chopped chives
4 T. butter
⅓ cup freshly grated Parmesan cheese

Directions: In a saucepan, warm the broth over low heat.

Warm 2 T. olive oil in a large saucepan over medium-high heat. Stir in the mushrooms, and cook until soft, about 3 minutes. Remove mushrooms and their liquid, and set aside.
Add 1 T. olive oil to skillet, and stir in the shallots. Cook 1 minute. Add rice, stirring to coat with oil, about 2 minutes. When the rice has taken on a pale, golden color, pour in wine, stirring constantly until the wine is fully absorbed. Add ½ cup broth to the rice, and stir until the broth is absorbed. Continue adding broth ½ cup at a time, stirring continuously, until the liquid is absorbed and the rice is al dente, about 15 to 20 minutes.
Remove from heat, and stir in mushrooms with their liquid, butter, chives, and Parmesan. Season with salt and pepper to taste.

Authentic Italian-style risotto must be cooked the slow and painful way, but oh so worth it. Complements grilled meats and chicken dishes very well. Check the rice by biting into it. It should be slightly al dente (or resist slightly to the tooth but not be hard in the center).

Tomatoes & Brie Cheese Pasta
For hot pasta

4-6 ripe tomatoes, cut into ½ inch cubes
1 lb. Brie cheese, rind removed, cut into irregular pieces
1 cup fresh basil, cut into strips with scissors

Marinade: 3 minced garlic cloves, ⅔ cup olive oil, 1 t. salt, ½ t. pepper, and crushed red pepper (optional)
Pour marinade over tomatoes, cheese, and basil. Mix well. Let stand, covered, for at least two hours at room temperature.
When ready to serve, pour over HOT pasta.

The heavier the sauce, the larger the noodle, so I suggest penne.

No man is lonely while eating spaghetti–it requires so much attention. ~ Anonymous

Notes

Casseroles
&
Side Dishes

Notes

Mom's Macaroni and Cheese

1 ½ cups elbow or macaroni of your choice cooked in salted water and drain…set aside
Melt in saucepan and whisk together
3 T. butter
2 T. flour
½ t. salt
Dash of pepper
Add 2 cups milk and cook until thick and bubbly
Add ½ cup finely chopped onion
Add 8 oz. sharp cheese, American or Cheddar, stirring until melted, fold in cooked macaroni
Pour mixture into a 1 ½ quart casserole
Some sprinkle breadcrumbs or Parmesan cheese on top before baking
Bake at 350 degrees for 35-45 minutes

Bul-Go-Ki

Korean: International party

In a large bowl, mix:
½ cup soy sauce
½ cup water
6 cloves garlic, chopped or crushed
3 green onions chopped
1 regular onion, sliced
2 T. sesame oil or vegetable oil
4 T. sugar
1-2 T. black pepper
Add 1 ½ to 2 lbs. of thinly sliced beef
Marinade for several hours then cook in a fry pan. Cooks quickly, maybe 10 minutes. Serve with rice.

Zucchini Pie

This is a wonderful dish, somewhat like a quiche, but also a veggie dish.

4 cups thinly sliced zucchini
1 cup chopped onion
½ cup butter
2 T. fresh parsley
½ t. salt
½ t. pepper
½ t. granulated garlic
¼ t. dried basil
¼ t. dried oregano
2 eggs (beaten)
8 oz. mozzarella or Parmesan cheese
8 oz. crescent rolls

Cook zucchini and onion in butter till tender (10 minutes)
Stir in seasonings
In a large bowl, blend eggs and cheese. Stir in veggies.
Separate crescent rolls into triangles and place in ungreased 10-inch pie pan.
Add the veggies
Bake at 375 degrees for 20-30 minutes

Broccoli Casserole

This recipe was my Thanksgiving responsibility for years, but now my sister-in-law, Wendy has been delighting the family table with her broccoli casserole.

Family size package of frozen broccoli, heat and drain
1 lb. Velvetta brand processed cheese and 1 stick butter
Pour into 9x13 casserole dish

Topping:
1 stick of butter
2 sleeves of Ritz Crackers crushed

When ready to bake, spread topping mix over broccoli. Bake at 350 degrees for 30-45 minutes or until topping is golden brown. *Best not to cover this dish after it comes out of the oven, as the topping can become soggy.*

Festive Onions
A great holiday dish to accompany turkey or ham.

Sauté: 4 cups thinly sliced onions (sweet onions are best) in 5 T. butter until transparent. Place in 8x8 glass baking dish
Beat: 2 eggs, then add 1 cup heavy cream
Salt and pepper
Pour over onions and sprinkle with ⅔ cup grated Parmesan cheese. Bake uncovered for approximately 25 minutes, at 350 degrees. *Use knife to test if done.*

When we moved to Florida the first holiday, the family lamented, "Who's going to make the festive onions at Thanksgiving?"

Italian Potato Pie
One of Doc's favorite dishes from his mother, Anne.

Melt:
2-3 T. butter in a round or square casserole dish with lid
Stir together:
Leftover mashed potatoes
2 eggs (beaten)
Fresh parsley and 1 t. granulated garlic
8-16 ounces of mozzarella cheese, cut into chunks (depending on the amount of leftover potatoes) and salami cut into small cubes (optional)
Top with melted butter and Parmesan cheese
Bake at 350 degrees until heated and cheese is melted, then remove lid and brown top the last few minutes.

Pizza Casserole
A true family favorite!

This pizza casserole is the recipe Barbara inquired about when I produced my three-ring binder of recipes that launched this cookbook!

Sauté:
1 medium onion (chopped) in 3 tablespoons of butter, place as bottom layer in a 11x13 glass casserole dish
Boil:
1 lb. spaghetti according to directions
1 package of sliced pepperoni (6-10 ounces)
Toss cooked pasta with sauce of your choice: *Don't skimp on the sauce...make it really juicy so the pasta will absorb the sauce. I use homemade or a combo of half Ragu and half Prego. My guess would be 8-9 cups total...So hold a cup or two out to serve with the heated casserole.*

Grated Cheeses: Mozzarella and Swiss cheese, equal amounts. *I am very generous with the cheeses...maybe a total 2 to 3 cups of each cheese.*
Layer: Place one half of the pasta & sauce on top of the onions, then ½ of the Swiss and ½ of the Mozzarella cheeses, then ½ of the pepperoni.
Repeat the layers...top with pepperoni. Bake at 350 degrees until bubbly. Approximately 30 minutes.
Serve with warm sauce

I always have extra sauce when I serve any type of pasta for those who love sauce...like me! I make this casserole days ahead, the longer is sits the better it gets. However, I try to get it out of the refrigerator so it's room temperature before I cook it. Everything is already cooked you are just trying to heat it thoroughly. When serving, try to cut in pieces like lasagna so that you are getting all the layers, not scooping off the top layer.

Sausage with Hot Peppers ala Tina
International Party

Brown 1 lb. sweet Italian turkey sausage, set aside
Brown ⅓ cup pine nuts – set aside

Start with ⅓ cup olive *(might add more)*
In skillet where sausage was cooked:
Add 2 medium shallots, cook for 2 minutes
Add 6 cloves minced garlic, cook for 1 minute
Add minced: 2 green habaneras, and 2 red jalapeño peppers, cook one more minute

Add 1 ½ to 2 cartons of cherry tomatoes, cut in halves
Add ¼ c raisins and the sautéed ⅓ c pine nuts
Bit of honey
Salt after each layer using very small amount of salt
Cook until the tomatoes start to break down, add sausage and serve.

Cathy's Baked Beans
An old-fashion picnic tradition that we've enjoyed for years

1 lb. bacon cut into small pieces before frying *(I use scissors to cut the bacon)*
When bacon is crispy drain grease and combine with the following:
3-4 medium size cans of baked beans
1 cup brown sugar
1 cup onion chopped, cooked in bacon grease
1 cup ketchup
½ t. dry mustard
Cook in crock pot all day or on stove top for several hours.

Bonnie's Baked Beans

Ingredients:
1 tall can of Bush's Best brand beans (32 oz)

Brown:
1 lb. bacon cut into small pieces
1 lb. ground beef
1 large onion, diced
1 green pepper, cut into small pieces

Add:
1 lb. of brown sugar
1 T. prepared mustard
1 large can of baked beans

Pour into a large pan and bake for three hours, stirring every ½ hour. The ingredients need to cook down to thicken. *Delicious!*

Sausage Casserole
The missionaries in Belize felt like royalty the morning I served this to them!

Mix:
6 eggs beaten
1 t. mustard
2 cups milk
1 t. salt
Set aside

Fold into mix:
6 slices of bread (cubed)
1 lb. ground sausage, fried and drained
4 oz. fresh mushrooms
2 cups grated Cheddar cheese

Pour bread mixture into a 9x13 pan. Pour egg mixture over it and bake at 350 degrees for 35-40 minutes. *Also good with 1 ½ cups of cubed ham chunks to replace the sausage meat.*

Yummy Potato Casserole

2 lb. frozen hash browns (thawed)
1 stick butter, melted
½ cup diced onion (sautéed)
1 t. salt & ¼ t. pepper
1 pint sour cream
1.5 or 2 cans cream of mushroom soup or cream of chicken soup
3 cups grated sharp cheddar cheese.
Combine ingredients then place in 9x13 pan and cover with crushed potato chips. *I once topped with corn flakes, but became a believer once I tasted it made with potato chips.*
Bake at 350 degrees for 45 minutes to 1 hour.

Corn Soufflé
Wonderful addition to Thanksgiving meal!

Mix:
1 can creamed style corn
1 can sweet corn (with juice)
1 box Jiffy corn bread
2 Eggs
1 package of 8 oz. cream cheese
Bake at 350 degrees in an ungreased 8x8 casserole for 20-30 minutes
For those who love heat, sometimes I add sliced jalapeños to half of the dish.

Italian Sausage and Peppers

Place sausage in pan with enough water to slightly cover. Puncture sausage with fork and cook on a low boil for 5 to 6 minutes, browning both sides. This can also be accomplished in a broiler.

In another pan, sauté 1 sliced green pepper, 1 onion quartered, add 2 crushed cloves of garlic, 1 t. oregano, with salt and pepper to taste.

Combine with cooked sausage, add quartered tomatoes and bake in over for 30 to 40 minutes.

I used to help my granddaddy make sausage. He would mix it up in a cleaned-out washtub with his hands, no gloves. Man, if we did anything like that today, they would jack the jail up and throw us under it. ~ Jimmy Dean

Celery Dressing for Turkey

Cut up 5 pieces of celery, 2-3 onions chopped, 3 eggs, 1 stick butter, 1 loaf of dried bread, cubed, 1 cup of Pepperidge farm dressing mix. Use lots of hot water and chicken broth. Salt and pepper to taste. Work together with your hands, it will be sloppy. Stuff into and around turkey and bake bird according to directions on label.

Thanksgiving dinners take eighteen hours to prepare. They are consumed in twelve minutes. Half-times take twelve minutes. This is not coincidence. ~ Erma Bombeck

Three Cheese Enchiladas

Ingredients:
1 ½ cups shredded Monterey Jack Cheese
1 ½ cups shredded cheddar cheese
1 package cream cheese, (3 oz.) softened
1 cup Picante brand salsa sauce
1 medium green or red bell pepper chopped
½ cup sliced green onions
1 t. crushed cumin
8 flour tortillas. Shredded lettuce, chopped tomato, sliced black olives
Combine: 1 cup of each cheese with softened cream cheese, ¼ cup salsa, pepper, onion, cumin and mix well.

Spoon ¼ cup cheese mixture across the center of each tortilla. Roll and place in pan, seam down in a 13x9 inch baking pan. Spoon remaining Picante sauce evenly over enchiladas; cover with remaining cheeses. Bake at 350 degrees for 20 minutes. Top with lettuce, tomato and black olives; serve with additional Picante, if desired.

Easy Cheese Enchilada
These are so yummy and easy, kids love them.

Sauté finely chopped onion in butter and set aside (non-stick skillet)
Place flour tortilla in same skillet (lightly buttered)
Sprinkle sharp Cheddar and Monterey Jack Cheese (equal amounts) on tortilla
Sprinkle sautéed onion, Mexican chopped chili peppers (these are not hot)
When tortilla is lightly browned and cheese is melted flip ½ over onto the other half
Remove from heat, cut into pie shaped pieces
Serve with sour cream, salsa, guacamole, jalapeños, or chopped tomatoes.

107

Sharon's Chili Rellenos

This casserole makes a nice addition to any brunch buffet.

2 cans green chilies (4 oz. size) Hot is best
2 cups Monterrey Jack cheese (shredded)
2 cups Colby or sharp cheese (shredded)
4 egg whites
4 egg yolks
⅔ cup evaporated milk
1 T. flour
1 t. salt
2 tomatoes, sliced

Remove seeds and dice up chilies. Mix with cheeses and pat in buttered 13x9 baking dish.
Beat:
4 egg whites until stiff, set bowl aside

Beat together:
4 egg yolks, milk, flour and salt. Fold in egg whites, then pour over cheese and chilies. Bake at 325 degrees for about 45 minutes.

Bubble and Squeak or Colcannon

British—International party

6 large potatoes-peeled and boiled until tender
½ head green cabbage- diced
1 cup onion- chopped
Salt, pepper, minced garlic
½ cup fresh parsley - chopped
3 T. butter

Melt the butter in a large frying pan and sauté onions until golden. Add diced cabbage and sauté until tender.
Meanwhile, make mashed potatoes with a bit of milk,

butter and seasonings of your choice. *Do not over mix or they will become gluey.* You can also use readymade potatoes from the grocery.

Gently fold onion, cabbage mix and parsley into potatoes. Then gently fold into buttered casserole dish. Cover and bake at 350 degrees until heated. Uncover and garnish with fresh herbs.

For a complete meal incorporate 2 cups of chopped ham or corned beef.

Wendy's Sweet Potato Casserole

1 large can sweet potatoes (drained and mashed)
2 eggs
⅓ cup sweet condensed milk
⅓ cup sugar
½ cup brown sugar
½ t. salt
½ t. vanilla
1 t. cinnamon
½ t. nutmeg
¼ t. ginger
⅓ cup melted butter
Mix above ingredients and place in a 8x8 inch baking dish

Topping:
Mix: 1 cup brown sugar
1 stick butter
½ cup flour
1 cup chopped pecans
Bake at 350 degrees for 30-40 minutes.

Sweet Potato Casserole

Combine:
3 cups cooked sweet potatoes, (usually 3) mashed well
1 cup sugar
½ cup melted butter
2 eggs, well beaten
1 t. Vanilla
⅓ cup milk

Stir well and spoon into 2-quart casserole

Topping:
½ cup brown sugar
¼ cup flour
2 ½ T. melted butter
½ cup pecans

Blend all ingredients until crumbly. Sprinkle on potato mixture. Bake at 350 degrees for 25 minutes. Garnish with marshmallows and put back into oven until brown.

Both sweet potato casseroles are delicious—one is more work the other is less work, so you pick!

Delicious Chicken Casserole
This recipe feeds a crowd!

Boil or bake 8-10 chicken breasts with skin and bone, then cool. Debone and skin and cut into bite size chunks.

I like to bake all my chicken recipes with the skin and bone because it gives the chicken more flavor.

Combine:
1 can Cream of Chicken soup

1 can Cream of Mushroom soup
1 cup mayonnaise
Mix with chicken pieces and place into a 11x13 glass
baking dish. Sprinkle with the ¾ cup blanched almonds

Topping:
Mix together the following ingredients:
1 cup of Pepperidge Farm stuffing mix
1 cup of crushed Wheatsworth brand crackers
Mix with 1 stick of melted butter

Spread topping on chicken mixture and bake 35-40 minutes
at 350 degrees.

Chicken Broccoli Vegetable Sauté

Ingredients:

4 chicken breasts (skinless & boneless)
1 whole broccoli bunch, cut up to flowerets
½ cup raw carrots, thinly sliced
1 cup fresh mushrooms, sliced in half
1 can cream of broccoli soup
⅓ cup of whole milk
⅛ t. pepper

Brown chicken in 1 T. butter till done, about five minutes
per side. Remove chicken and keep warm.
Using same skillet and remaining butter, sauté broccoli,
carrots and mushrooms for about 5 minutes, stirring often.
Stir together undiluted soup, milk and pepper before adding
to skillet. Heat to boiling before returning chicken to
skillet. Reduce heat to low and simmer for five minutes.

Curry Chicken Casserole

Ingredients:
6 chicken breasts (boneless) browned in oil
2 cups fresh broccoli flowerets layered on buttered casserole dish. Place cooked chicken on top.

Mix:
2 ½ cups cream of chicken soup
1 ½ cup mayonnaise
⅔ cup half and half cream

Add:
1 ½ cup Cheddar cheese shredded
2 t. lemon juice
¼ to 1 t. curry powder
Combine all ingredients, pour over chicken. Cover with buttered breadcrumbs bake at 350 degrees for 40 minutes.

Beef Stroganoff

2 ½ lbs of filet of beef cut into thin strips, trimming the fat
4 T. butter
2 T. vegetable oil
½ lb. of fresh mushrooms, sliced
3 T. minced shallots or green onions
½ cup sweet sherry
¼ cup beef broth
1 ¾ t. black pepper
1 cup sour cream

Heat 2 T. butter and 1 T. oil in a large skillet. Sauté mushrooms for 3 minutes, add onions for 2 more minutes. Remove from skillet and set aside. Add remaining butter and oil. Over high heat cook the beef. Remove cooked meat and drain off oil.

Add the sherry to deglaze the pan, scraping bottom well. Add broth to cook for 2 minutes. Season meat with salt and pepper and return to skillet with the mushrooms. Cover and continue cooking on high heat for 5 minutes, stirring frequently. Just before serving add sour cream but do not boil.

Serve over buttered noodles or other favorite pasta.

Cathy's Beef Stew
The canned onions make this dish!

2 lbs of beef cubes browned in 2 T. oil
Add:
1 can cream of mushroom soup
1 can golden mushroom soup
½ can of water
1 T. Worcestershire sauce

Cover and simmer for 2 hours.

Add:
6 carrots, cut in 2 inch pieces
8 oz. jar of Thank You Brand white onions, (mix in blender)

After 1 hour add:
1 package frozen green beans, (thawed) continue simmering for 30 more minutes, stirring occasionally. Thicken sauce if desired. Serve over buttered noodles.

Nothing ever tastes bad with a little extra cheese on top, it just never hurt a thing in its life. ~ Paula Deen

Steamed Broccoli

You will not believe how simple and delicious this dish is!
Now that's Italian!

In a large soup pan sauté 6 cloves finely chopped garlic in
3 T. olive oil *(Do Not Burn)*
Once garlic is lightly browned add: broccoli flowerets, salt
and pepper and 1 cup steaming HOT water.
Immediately cover and steam for 5 minutes, or until tender.
Remove broccoli and top with the bits of garlic and serve.

*The sudden burst of steam infuses the broccoli and your
taste buds will surely dance!*

Foolproof Beef & Broccoli

Ingredients:
¾ lb. boneless beef sirloin steak
1 T. vegetable oil
1 clove garlic, minced
1 medium onion, cut into wedges
1 can Cream of Broccoli soup
¼ cup water
1 T. soy sauce
2 cups broccoli flowerets

Hot cooked noodles

Slice sirloin steak into thin strips and fry in hot oil with
garlic until browned.
Add onion and continue cooking for 5 minutes, stirring
often.
Mix together soup, water and soy sauce and add to skillet
and heat till boiling before adding broccoli. Reduce heat to
low, cover and simmer for 5 minutes or until broccoli is
tender. Serve over hot noodles. *Don't overcook the
broccoli!*

Green Pancakes ala Tony

Ingredients:
15 eggs…beat first
Mix in:
1 ¼ cup Parmesan cheese
2 cups flour
Salt and pepper to taste
Granulated garlic and crushed red pepper *(see my hints about these two ingredients) Page 162*

Add:
2 packages of frozen spinach thawed completely, squeeze out water till nearly dry…20 ounces total.

Mix again…should be the consistency of pancake batter. Use scant ¼ cup batter and pour into hot oil and prepare like potato pancakes. Drain on paper towels, and sprinkle with salt after removing from oil. *Super Yummy!*

My buddy Tony usually cooks for a crowd, so I often cut this recipe in half. Our 2-year old grandson, Aiden, loves these pancakes! They have become a nice addition to our Christmas Eve buffet. This dish serves as a bread but also a veggie. They also keep nicely in the refrigerator for a few days.

I do not like broccoli. And I haven't liked it since I was a little kid and my mother made me eat it. And I'm President of the United States and I'm not going to eat any more broccoli.~ President George W. Bush (1990)

Eggplant Parmesan

Ingredients:
Favorite Red Sauce (homemade or commercial)
3 medium size eggplant…*I also love the baby eggplant for special occasions*
Breading:
3 ½ cups Italian breadcrumbs
½ cup Parmesan cheese
2 T. granulated garlic
1 T. oregano
1 t. crushed red pepper
Egg wash:
6 eggs and ½ cup milk
*Flour
Fresh Mozzarella Cheese 1-2 lbs depending on your love of cheese.

Peel eggplant *(some prefer not to peel, but I always peel)* and cut into ½ to ¼ inch rounds, soak in salt water for 30 minutes while preparing the breadcrumbs and egg mixture.
In a flat dish combine all the breading ingredients.
Prepare egg wash in flat dish (pie pan)
*Place flour in a zip lock bag or flat dish
Prepare a cookie sheet lined with paper towels for the cooked eggplant, to drain the grease.
Pat eggplant with paper towel, dip into flour, then egg mixture and finally into breadcrumb mixture.
Fry in hot canola or vegetable oil, drain on paper towels.
When all eggplant is fried, pour about 1-2 cups of spaghetti sauce in the bottom of a 9X13 casserole dish.
Layer a piece of eggplant, then a sliced of fresh mozzarella cheese, another piece of eggplant and top with sauce. You can sprinkle grated cheese on top also.
Can be frozen or made a day ahead of time. I find if I have the casserole at room temperature before I bake it, the dish works better. Bake at 350 degrees for approximately 30-45

minutes. I always make my homemade sauce several days before using it.

This dish is some work, but it is so worth it. One evening in Florida, some of my girlfriends got together and we made this dish. Of course, a few days earlier we made the homemade sauce. When we finished everyone got a portion of the eggplant to take home to share with their hubbies for dinner. What fun we had! I'm convinced that cooking together is much more fun than cooking alone. Invite close friends for dinner and then prepare your meal together!

Green Bean Casserole
Thanksgiving wouldn't be complete without this dish

Blend:
2 cans cream of mushroom soup
1 cup milk
2 t. soy sauce
¼ t. pepper
Stir soup and milk over medium heat before adding the soy sauce, and pepper

Add:
8 cups cooked green beans
1 ⅓ cup French's Fried Onion Rings (The can holds 2 ⅔ cups, so save the last cup for topping).
Pour into a 3-quart casserole dish
Bake at 350 degrees for 25 minutes, or until bubbly hot…Stir
Topping:
1 cup French's French Fried Onions and bake for 10 minutes longer.

Three Quick and Easy Cold Veggies

*We've always served olives, both green and black. So here
are three separate variations that our kids have loved over
the years*

*   *   *

1 can black olives pitted *(the kids would put olives on their
fingers and eat them one at a time)*
1 can green beans
Toss with Italian Dressing, serve chilled

*   *   *

1 bottle large green olives with pits
Celery stalks, cut into pieces
Toss with my homemade Italian dressing, serve chilled

*   *   *

Cauliflower
Broccoli
Mini carrots
Cut into small pieces, toss with Italian dressing. Let this set
for an hour to marinate, serve chilled.

*Onions and bacon cooking up just makes your kitchen
smell so good. In fact, one day I'm going to come up with a
room deodorizer that smells like bacon and onions. It's a
fabulous smell. ~Paula Deen*

Breads

Notes

Bob Furci's Pizza Dough

All ingredients are approximate:
4-5 pounds of unbleached flour (not self-rising)
Dissolve 2 packages of dry yeast in 1½ quarts of warm water (not too hot)
1 ½ T. salt and 2 T. sugar
3 caps full of olive oil
Start with water and yeast, stirring, then add other ingredients except flour. When yeast is dissolved, start working the flour into the liquid one handful at a time. When dough begins to separate from the sides of bowl, take out to grease the bottom of bowl. Place back in bowl and cover with a clean, damp dishtowel for two hours at room temperature. Divide dough in half to form 1-1 ½ lb. balls. Wrap in plastic wrap and refrigerate until ready to use.

Strombolli
We've enjoyed this fabulous party food for years!

Roll pizza dough out to a large rectangle, about 10 x 14 in. Use homemade or some pizza's places sell raw dough. Spread the following three layers of deli meat within one-inch of the edges:
Boiled or baked ham (medium sliced). Italian-style capicola ham (mild or spicy). Italian salami (we like sopressata) but can use any Italian salami
Layer cheeses:
Provolone slices, medium or thick and sprinkle mozzarella
Roll dough into a cylinder tucking in the sides before you begin to roll, pinching the ends to seal.
Use egg wash to seal the seam and brush the top, then place on baking sheet seam down.
Bake at 350 degrees for 20-30 minutes or until golden brown. Let set 10 minutes before cutting.
Optional: pepperoni, hot peppers, pizza sauce, Parmesan cheese. Slice in 2-inch servings.

Anne's Italian Pork Biscuits
Doc's Italian mother gave me this recipe.

Make "Chitlins":
Chop up one pork chop in tiny pieces using fat as well.
Cook until very crisp. Set Aside

Dissolve: 4 packs of dry yeast dissolved in ¾ cup warm water

Add:
6-8 cups All Purpose flour
1 T. black pepper
1 T. salt
¾ cup lard

Mix by hand…Add more water while mixing about ½ cup, but add slowly.
Cover with towel and allow dough to rise. When doubled in size, stir it up again and then add chitlins mixing again and allowing to rise once more.

Prepare biscuits. Roll dough into long pieces and cut into app. 5 inch pieces. Form a circle by lapping over one end of the dough piece and squeeze down to keep from separating during baking. Bake at 325 degrees for approximately 45 minutes.

These crunchy biscuits were always a special treat that Don's mother made for us each time we visited her. I had no idea how much work they involved until I started making them on my own for our family. I don't prepare them often but what a treat when I do!

Sharon's Almond Poppy Seed Bread

Mix the following ingredients with an electric mixer:

2 ¼ cup of sugar
3 eggs
1 ⅛ cup vegetable oil
1 ½ cups of milk

Add:
3 cups flour
½ t. salt
1 ½ t. baking powder
1 ½ t. almond flavoring
1 ½ t. butter flavoring
1 ½ t. vanilla
1 ½ t. poppy seeds

Bake in two greased and floured loaf pans at 350 degrees for one hour or if using mini loaf pans, bake for 50 minutes.

Anne's Banana Nut Bread
This is super moist and freezes well

Combine:
⅓ cup vegetable shortening or butter
1 ½ cup sugar
2 cups all purpose flour
1 ½ t. baking soda
3 overripe bananas – the riper the better
1 cup chopped nuts such a pecans or walnuts

Mix in order. Grease and flour-dust two loaf pans. Bake at 350 degrees for 40-50 minutes.

Mamma Renzetti's Focaccia Bread

2 ⅔ cups all purpose flour
1 t. salt
1 t. white sugar
1 packet of active dry yeast (14 ounce)
1 t. garlic powder
1 t. oregano
½ t. dried basil
1 dash black pepper
1 t. vegetable oil
2 T. olive oil
2 T. Parmesan cheese (grated)
1 ½ cups mozzarella cheese (shredded)

Directions: Mix the yeast and warm water in a small bowl. Let proof for 10 minutes (until bubbles begin to form).

In a large bowl, stir together flour, salt, sugar, garlic powder, oregano, thyme, basil and black pepper.

Add the yeast mix and vegetable oil to the dry ingredients and combine.

When dough has pulled together, turn out onto lightly floured surface and knead until smooth and elastic.

Lightly oil a large bowl, place dough in bowl, and turn to coat with oil Cover with a damp cloth and let rise in a warm place for 25 minutes.

Preheat oven to 425 degrees.

Punch dough down, place on greased baking sheet. Pat dough into ½ thick rectangle *(doesn't have to be perfect)*. Using your knuckle, make indentations in the dough about ½ apart, then prick the dough with fork.

Brush top with olive oil, then sprinkle with Parmesan and mozzarella cheese. Bake for 13-15 minutes until golden brown.

This classic Italian bread is inspired by the late Mamma Renzetti and her former family owned grocery chain in Columbus. She was a gracious Christian lady who was a wonderful cook and great hostess.

Moist Carrot Bread Mold
This dish serves both as a bread and vegetable.

Combine:
½ cup butter (1 stick)
1 cup brown sugar
1 egg
1 ¼ cup flour
1 t. baking powder
½ t. baking soda
1 T. lemon juice
1 T. water
½ t. nutmeg
½ t. cinnamon
½ t. salt
1 cup grated raw carrots

Mix as a cake. Pour into a greased ring mold for 30 minutes at 375 degrees.

Good bread is the most fundamentally satisfying of all foods; and good bread with fresh butter, the greatest of feasts. ~ James Beard

Pumpkin Bread

2 cups mashed pumpkin from can
3 ½ cups flour
4 eggs beaten
2 t. baking soda
1 cup oil
1 ½ t. salt
3 cups sugar
1 t. nutmeg
1 t. cinnamon
⅔ cup cold water

Mix ingredients together. Pour into 2 greased loaves pans. Bake at 350 degrees for 70 minutes. Let cool in pans for 15-20 minutes. Wrap in plastic wrap to keep fresh.

Biscotti

Cream:
1 stick butter, softened
1 cup sugar

Beat in:
3 eggs (2 whole and 1 white, save the remaining yolk)

Sift together:
2 ¼ to 2 ½ cups of All Purpose flour
2 *heaping* teaspoons baking powder

Later: 2 T. Anise seed (heaping)

Stir in flour and Anise seeds to form soft dough. Separate the dough into four equal parts. Working on a well-floured board, form 4 rolls the size of fat sausages.

Brush with remaining yoke and bake for about 20 to 25 minutes in a 350-degree oven.

Remove from oven and slice ½ inch cookies, cutting diagonally, with a serrated bread knife. Place back in oven to toast for about 5 to 10 minutes to become crisp. Cool on rack.

Ultimate Coffee Cake

Ingredients:
16 to 18 unbaked frozen dinner rolls (balls)
1 package (3-ounce) regular Butterscotch pudding mix, (not instant)
½ cup brown sugar, packed
½ cup pecans, chopped
1 stick-butter, melted

Directions: The night before place frozen rolls in well greased Bundt pan. Sprinkle dry pudding mix over rolls. Sprinkle brown sugar over pudding mix. Sprinkle chopped pecans over brown sugar. Pour melted butter over all. To prevent the dough from forming a hard crust while its rising overnight, cover with a damp towel or tightly wrap with plastic wrap. Let rise overnight at room temperature, about 5 hours or possibly longer. Can thaw in refrigerator overnight. Preheat oven to 350 degrees.

Bake in oven for 30 minutes. Remove from the oven and allow to cool for 5 minutes. Turn pan over onto a serving platter to remove. Serve by pulling apart chunks with fingers.

This coffee cake is great served for out-of-town company or on Christmas morning with the kids!

Notes

Desserts

Notes

Easy Mini Cheese Cakes

Combine:
3 packages of cream cheese, softened (8 oz. size)
1 cup sugar
3 eggs
1 t. vanilla

Using muffin tins, place a vanilla wafer cookie in a small cupcake liner for the crust. Fill each cup ¾ full and bake at 350 degrees for 20 minutes.

Cheese Fingers

Super easy and so good...Absolutely one of our favorite desserts!

Mix 1st layer:
1 package yellow cake mix
1 stick melted butter
1 egg
Spread into 9x13 in baking dish, press lightly
Blend 2nd layer:
8 oz. cream cheese
2 eggs
3 cups powdered sugar
Pour on first layer, bake at 325 degrees for 40-60 minutes.

Fruit Dip

Blend:
1 package cream cheese (8 oz. size)
1 small jar marshmallow cream
4 T. lemon juice of fresh lemon
Serve with assorted fruits: strawberries, bananas, pears, apples, pineapple, or grapes. Also good served with pound cake or banana bread.

Nestle Toll House Pan Cookies

Blend:
1 cup butter, softened
¾ cup sugar
¾ cup brown sugar
1 t. vanilla

Beat in:
2 eggs
Sift together and gradually add:
2 ¼ cup un-sifted flour
1 t. baking soda
1 t. salt
Stir in nuts and chocolate chip morsels. Spread cookie dough mixture onto a greased 10 x15 jellyroll pan. Bake at 375 degrees for 20 to 25 minutes. Cool slightly then cut into 2-inch squares. Yields about 35 squares.

Ladyfinger Cake

2-3 packages readymade Ladyfingers
1 pint heavy cream
2 packages cream cheese (8 oz)
¾ cups sugar
1 t. vanilla
Line sides and bottom of a 10' spring form pan with ladyfingers, set aside.

Whip the heavy cream until stiff, set side.
Mix the softened cream cheese until smooth. Add the sugar a tablespoon at a time, mixing well. Next, add the vanilla. Fold in the whipped cream to the creamed cheese mixture, blending thoroughly.
Spoon *half* the filling mixture into the ladyfinger lined pan. Cover with a layer of ladyfingers. Next add remainder of filling.

Wait until you're ready to serve before adding the topping.

Topping:
2 quarts of fresh strawberries
2 T. cornstarch to thicken (optional)
Mash thoroughly about a cup of berries, heating over medium heat. Mix cornstarch with a little water, add to pan stirring until thickened. Add rest of berries, stirring well. Cool before serving.

Perfect Peach Cobbler

3 cups fresh or canned peaches
Spread peaches in bottom of a 10x7x1 inch-baking pan.
Sprinkle with 1 T. lemon juice

Sift together:
1 cup flour
1 cups sugar
½ t. salt
Add 1 beaten egg, and toss until crumbly. Sprinkle over peaches, then drizzle with 6 T. melted butter
Bake at 375 degrees for 35-40 minutes. Serve warm with ice cream.

After a good dinner one can forgive anybody, even one's own relatives. ~ Oscar Wilde

Luscious Cake

1 yellow cake mix plus ingredients to prepare
1 can crushed pineapple (20 oz.)
1 ⅓ cups sugar
1 French instant vanilla pudding, (large box size) plus ingredients to prepare pudding
1 ½ cups heavy cream
1 cup flaked, sweetened toasted coconut.

Bake the cake according to directions in a 13x9 inch pan

Combine:
Crushed pineapple and 1 cup sugar in a sauce pan, bring to boil over medium heat stirring constantly. Remove from heat and cool slightly.

Remove cake from oven, use fork to pierce holes into cake. Pour pineapple mixture over hot cake and set aside.

Prepare pudding according to package directions. Spread pudding over cake and refrigerate until thoroughly chilled.

Whip heavy cream and remaining sugar until stiff. Cover top of cake with whipped cream and toasted coconut.

Moist Chocolate Cake

Mix:
1 package pudding-style box chocolate cake mix
1 cup mayonnaise
1 cup water
3 eggs

Pour batter into a greased 9 x 13 inch pan. Bake at 350 degrees for 30 to 35 minutes.

Fabulous Chocolate Cake

1 box Pillsbury chocolate cake mix (do not prepare)
1 Thank You brand cherry pie filling (16 oz.)
1 T. almond extract
2 eggs

Mix together all ingredients by hand and pour into a 9x13 greased cake pan. Bake at 350 degrees for 20 to 30 minutes.

Chocolate Icing

Prepare:
1 cup sugar
5 T. butter
⅓ cup milk
Bring this mixture to a boil and remove from heat. Stir in 6 oz. chocolate chips. Spread over cooled cake.

Graham Cracker Pralines
Probably my most requested dessert recipe!

1 cup butter
1 cup brown sugar
Boil 2 minutes, remove from heat and add 1 t. vanilla and 1 cup chopped pecans. Stir.

Pour immediately over graham crackers placed on a jelly roll pan (20-24 crackers broken into four parts). Bake at 300 degrees for 8-10 minutes.
*Immediately remove from pan and cool on racks or waxed paper. *This is important to keep praline bars from sticking.*

Chocolate Chip – Oatmeal Cookies

Beat together:
1 cup margarine or butter
1 ½ cup packed brown sugar
½ cup sugar
2 t. vanilla
2 T. milk

Sift together:
1 ¼ cup all purpose flour
1 t. baking soda
1 t. salt

Combine:
2 ½ cups Quaker brand quick oats (or old fashion)
12 oz. Nestle Toll House semi-sweet chocolate chips
1 cup chopped nuts
Add flour to wet mixture and mix well before adding oats, chips and nuts. Drop by rounded teaspoon onto un-greased cookie sheet. Bake at 375 degrees for 9-10 minutes for chewy or 11-12 minutes for a crisper cookie. Yield: 5 dozen cookies.

Texas Sheet Cake & Icing
My favorite chocolate cake!

Combine in saucepan:
1 cup butter
1 cup water
4 T. unsweetened cocoa powder
Bring to a boil and remove from heat.

Add and mix with electric mixer:
2 cups sugar
2 cups flour

½ t. baking soda
2 eggs
½ cup sour cream
1 t. vanilla

Pour into a greased and floured jellyroll pan. Bake at 350 degrees for about 20 minutes.

Icing for Texas Sheet Cake

In a saucepan:
Melt ¼ cup butter with 4 T. unsweetened cocoa powder, remove from heat.

Add the following ingredients, blending with a mixer:
4 cups powdered sugar and 6 T. whole milk, along with 1 t. vanilla. Mix well before adding 1 cup chopped walnuts or pecans. Spread chocolate icing mix on top of hot cake as soon as it comes from the oven. This forms a fudge-like layer.
If taking this cake to a gathering, I omit the nuts on half of the icing for the benefit of those with nut allergies of any kind.

Carmel Icing

For a chocolate cake, my favorite childhood birthday cake combination

Melt 1 stick of butter
1 cup brown sugar
Cook for approximately 5 minutes
Add 1 box 10x sugar and slowly adding 4-5 T. milk to correct consistency. Beat with mixer until smooth.

Fabulous Salted Peanut Chews

Base:
1 package Pillsbury "plus" yellow cake mix
¾ cup margarine or butter softened
1 egg
3 cups miniature marshmallows

Topping:
⅔ cup corn syrup
¼ cup margarine or butter
2 t. vanilla
12 oz (2 cups) peanut butter chips
2 cups crisp rice cereal
2 cups salted peanuts

Combine base ingredients except marshmallows.

Mix at low speed until crumbly. Press into 9 x13 pan. Bake at 350 degrees 12 to 18 minutes, or until golden brown.

Remove from oven and sprinkle with marshmallows, return to oven for two minutes. Cool.

Heat the corn syrup, butter, vanilla and peanut butter chips until melted and smooth, stirring constantly. Remove from heat and fold in the rice cereal and peanuts, immediately spoon over cookie base. Cut into bars when room temperature. Store covered and chilled.

One year I made these labor-intensive cookies, which were expensive as well, for a Christmas cookie exchange. Can you guess my reaction when a woman waltzed through the door carrying a few bags of store bought cookies? I was not a happy camper! C'est La Vie!

Cherries in the Snow
Use a glass truffle for this dish

For bottom layer, mix together:
1 pkg. cream cheese (8 oz.)
½ cup sugar
½ cup milk
Next layer: 1 container light cool whip (8 oz size)
Next layer: 1 Angel food cake, torn into pieces.
Top with 1 can cherry pie filling and cool at room
temperature for 3 hours.

Apple Kuchen

1 pkg. yellow cake mix
1 stick of soft butter
½ cup of flaked coconut
Mix and pat into an ungreased 13x9-baking dish, building
up around the edges. Bake for 10 minutes at 350 degrees.
Arrange 2 ½ cups of sliced baking apples (peeled) on warm
crust. Optional: Can use canned pie filling.
Mix:
½ cup sugar and 1 t. cinnamon and sprinkle over apples.
Blend 1 cup sour cream with 1 egg. Drizzle over apples and
bake for another 25 minutes. Do not over bake. Serve
warm. *I love it with ice cream!*

This recipe can be made with white cake mix and 1 can
sliced peaches drained (29 oz. size).

*I first tasted this at a ladies card club and asked for the
recipe! So easy and delicious!*

Heidi's Cherry Strudel

In a saucepan, melt: 2 cups unsalted butter (set aside)

In a bowl, combine:
1 cup sugar
1 cup corn flake crumbs
1 t. ground cinnamon

Filling:
1 can Thank You brand cherry pie filling (16 oz)
1 t. Amaretto liqueur
½ t. almond flavoring

Dough: Athens strudel leaves. Thaw before using.
Butter clean counter top, working fast. Cover remaining leaves with damp pastry cloth to keep from drying out.

*Lay one sheet of dough on buttered counter, liberally "flick" melted butter on dough with pastry brush, carefully. Dough will tear easily. Continue process, buttering each layer until you've done 4-6 layers.

Put half of the cherry filling on the first strudel. Start to roll, tucking edges, continuing to roll until end. Butter log, sprinkle with sugar mix, cut before baking, but don't cut all the way through. Bake at 375 degrees for 20 minutes. For an apple filling strudel, use an orange flavored liqueur.

*See Susan's Hints on handling this dough

In the back of the book under "Tidbits About Susan," be sure to read the "Pass the Charred Chicken," a funny story that mentions this recipe. (Page 171)

Taffy Apple Pizza

I thank the Bockrath family for introducing me to this refreshing dessert.

Shape 1 package refrigerated sugar cookie dough on pizza pan or baking stone. Bake at 350 degrees for 16-18 minutes or until golden brown.
Remove and cool 10 minutes.
Loosen from pan with spatula
Combine:
1 cream cheese (8 oz.)
½ cup brown sugar
¼ cup creamy peanut butter
½ t. vanilla
Mix well then spread evenly over cookie
Peel and core Granny Smith apples and cut in half pieces and arrange over cookie
Drizzle ¼ cup caramel ice cream topping (soften in microwave)
Sprinkle ½ cup chopped peanuts.

Cherry-Pineapple Jell-O

1 large box cherry Jell-O brand
1 large can cherry pie filling
1 can crushed pineapple

Dissolve jell-o packages in 2 cups of boiling water. Drain pineapple—add to jell-o, then fold in cherry pie filling.

Pour mixture into a 9x13 dish and refrigerate. Frost with 1 tub of Cool Whip (8 oz) and top with crushed nuts (optional).

I got hooked on this at one our pool parties...such a refreshing summer dessert!

Carrot Cake I

2 cups sifted flour
1 t. salt
2 t. baking soda
2 t. cinnamon
1 t. vanilla
3 or 4 ounces of Angel flake coconut
¼ cup chopped pecans
1 cup chopped dates
1 ¼ cup light oil
1 cup water
2 cups sugar
4 eggs, room temperature
Approximately 5 carrots shredded

Put carrots in food processor or blender with 1 cup of water. If using a blender, do in smaller portions at a time. After shredding, place carrots in a colander to drain off excess water.
Sift together flour, soda, salt and cinnamon. Set aside.
Add all other ingredients, mixing well before pouring into a greased 9 x13 in pan. Bake at 325-350 degrees for 55-60 minutes
Cool before frosting with cream cheese icing.

Cream Cheese Frosting

Cream together:
1 stick butter, softened
1 package cream cheese, (8 oz.) softened
1 t. vanilla
Add:
1 box powdered sugar. *(Don't add the whole box at once in case it's too stiff. Gradually add the confection sugar)*

Carrot Cake II

Ingredients:
4 eggs
1 ½ cups vegetable oil
2 cups flour
2 t. baking soda
2 t. baking powder
1 ½ t. salt
2 t. ground cinnamon
2 cups sugar
1 8-oz crushed pineapple, drain juice
2 cups packed shredded carrots
½ cup chopped nuts

Blend eggs and oil in a large mixing bowl.
Sift flour and dry ingredients together before adding to wet mixture, add sugar and mix well before adding pineapple, carrots and nuts. Pour into a greased 9 x13 inch-baking pan. Bake at 350 degrees for 45 to 55 minutes or until cake tests done.

Mom's Butter Balls

My buddy, Mike Singer, affectionately calls these diet pills!

Cream:
1 cup butter softened
¾ cup powdered sugar
1 t. vanilla
⅛ t. almond extract
Add:
2 cups flour
1 cup finely chopped pecans

Form into small balls and bake on ungreased cookie sheet at 350 degrees for 20 minutes. Roll in powdered sugar immediately—store when cooled completely.

Rolled Sugar Cookies

Cream:
1 cup margarine or butter
1 ½ cup white sugar

Add:
3 eggs, one egg at a time to mix well
1 t. almond extract
1 t. vanilla

Sift together:
3 cups of flour
1 t. baking soda
1 t. cream of tartar

After thoroughly mixed, refrigerate for at least 3 hours. Take out an amount to roll out, leaving the rest of the dough refrigerated.

Roll out on a flour pasty cloth and cut into desired cookie shapes. Bake at 375 degrees for 7 to 8 minutes.

Icing for Decorated Sugar Cookies

3 cups of powdered sugar
½ stick butter
¼ t. vanilla
½ t. almond extract
Add 1 t. of milk at a time till the right consistency to frost cookies. Sprinkle with candies.

Fun to do with the grandkids! I must admit I have been known to purchase cut out cookies from the bakery and let them have a blast icing them!

Christmas Spritz Cookies

Cream:
1 cup shortening or butter
¾ cup sugar
Add:
1 egg
1 t. vanilla
Sift together before adding:
2 ¼ cup all purpose flour
½ t. baking powder and add a pinch of salt
Use an array of food coloring to tint each batch.

Blend well and fill cookie press and select design. Bake on un-greased cookie sheet at 400 degrees for 10 to 12 minutes. Yield: 5-dozen cookies.

Layered Chocolate Brownie Mousse
For an impressive dessert, use a glass truffle bowl.

Ingredients:
2 packages Jello-O chocolate instant pudding (3.9 oz.), prepared according to package directions.
5 tubs (8 oz.) Cool Whip brand whipped topping (thawed)
1 box brownie mix prepared, torn into 1-inch chunks
Mousse:
Mix 2 tubs of the Cool Whip with the prepared pudding.
Start the layers: 1st layer is plain Cool Whip then randomly place brownie chunks
Add a layer of the mouse, followed by brownie chunks
Top with 2nd layer of Cool Whip, then mouse followed by a 3rd layer of plain Cool Whip.
Lastly, sprinkle your favorite candy bar pieces or chocolate shavings or top with fresh raspberries.

Martha's Oatmeal Cookies

Cream:
1 cup butter
¾ cup white sugar
¾ cup brown sugar

Add 1 egg and 1 t. vanilla

Add:
1 cup dried cherries
1 cup chocolate chips
1 cup toffee chips (Skor or Heath candy bits)

Form three logs, wrap in plastic wrap. After chilling till firm, cut in 1 ½ inch slices. Bake at 350 degrees for 8 to 10 minutes.

Doris' Kooky Cookies
Fabulous as appetizer or dessert!

Lightly butter jellyroll pan
Spread original size Fritos (10.5 ounces) on cookie sheet

Combine:
1 cup sugar
1 cup light Karo syrup
Bring to a rolling boil and remove from heat
Add 1 cup peanut butter and stir until blended (smooth or chunky)

Drizzle over Fritos and cool
Break into small portions to serve

Raspberry Jell-O

Combine:
1 large box of raspberry Jell-O
2 cups boiling water, stirring well. Set aside to cool to room temperature.

Add:
2 packages of frozen raspberries
1 jar of applesauce (15 ounces)

Refrigerate until set. Serve with real whipped cream.

Sharon's Chocolate Chip Cookies

Cream:
1 cup butter flavored Crisco brand shortening
¾ cup white sugar
¾ cup brown sugar
1 t. vanilla

Add:
2 eggs, beaten

Mix:
1 t. soda
1 t. salt
2 ¼ cups flour

Add to shortening mixture and blend well before adding 12 ounces of chocolate chips. Drop by teaspoons and bake at 375 degrees for 8 minutes. Do not over bake for chewy cookies. Yield: 6-dozen cookies.

Jimilea's Peanut Butter Fudge

Combine:
3 cups of sugar
⅔ cup evaporated milk
1 ½ stick of butter
In a heavy saucepan on medium heat, bring to a boil for 5 minutes

Add:
1 cup peanut butter
1 jar of marshmallow (7 oz.)
1 t. vanilla
Mix till these ingredients dissolve then pour into a buttered pan and cool.

Wayne's Tiramisu

Combine:
1 cup sugar and 3 T. cornstarch
Separate 6 eggs, (use only yolks)
Mix sugar and cornstarch. Whisk egg yolks, then add to cornstarch mixture.

Heat:
2 ½ cups half and half until steaming. Add sugar mixture slowly, small amount at a time, stirring constantly. Return to heat after all is blended and cook for about 5 minutes, or until thickens then remove from heat.

Add: 2 cups Mascarpone Cheese and blend well.

Blend ¾ cup very strong coffee… *(I used instant)* with 3 T. Kahlau
Drag through or pour over ladyfingers. (Approximately 2 packages) Line a 9 x13 baking dish with fingers.

Hint: If your ladyfingers are hardened you can drag them through the coffee mixture. If they are soft you will have to spoon coffee over them.

Cover the Lady Fingers with ½ of the pudding mixture…add another layer of Lady Fingers…then the remaining pudding mixture.
Let cool before doing the top layer
Top Layer:
Beat 1 cup whipping cream until stiff, add 3 T. sugar, ½ t. vanilla.
Spread over top layer and sprinkle with shaved chocolate or cocoa powder.

Shelly's "Shaw" Popcorn

Melt 2 sticks of butter
½ cup corn syrup
2 cups brown sugar
1 t. salt
Bring to a rolling boil for 5 minutes
(Prepare 2 disposable baking pans with Pam spray)
Add 1 t. baking soda and 1 t. vanilla to caramel mix
Pour over 1 ½ bags (½ in each pan) of Mike Sells brand of Hulless popcorn, stirring well *(purchased in any supermarket)*
Bake at 250 degrees for 1 hour stirring every 15 minutes
Can add toasted pecans for a real treat.

Let us always meet each other with a smile, for a smile is the beginning of love. We shall never know all the good a simple can do. ~ Mother Theresa

Don's Mom's Cheese Cake

Blend:
1 cup Graham cracker crumbs
1 t. vanilla
3 T. butter, melted
Pat on bottom of 9 x13 baking dish
Combine:
2 packages of cream cheese, softened (8 oz.)
4 large eggs
1 sour cream container (16 oz.)
1 cup sugar
1 t. vanilla
Spread over Graham cracker crust and sprinkle with nutmeg. Bake at 350 degrees for 45 minutes. Turn off oven and allow to "set" in oven for about one hour.

Wonderful Cheese Cake

This cheesecake is always a crowd pleaser and I believe the pecan nuts in the crust are the reason. It's a little more work than other cheesecakes, but well worth it.

Crust:
16 double graham crackers, crushed
1 ½ T. sugar
4 T. butter
½ cup finely chopped pecans
Mix all ingredients together until blended. Place in 13x9 in glass baking dish, set aside

Filling:
3 packages cream cheese (8 oz.) softened
5 eggs
1 cup sugar
1 ½ t. vanilla
Beat softened cheese with electric beaters until smooth. Add eggs one at a time and beat well. Add sugar and

vanilla. Cream well.

Pour onto crust. Bake at 300 degrees for 1 hour or until toothpick comes out clean

Topping:

1 ½ pints sour cream

½ cup sugar

Allow cake to cool for 5 minutes after baking before topping. Mix ingredients well and put on top of cake. Return to oven for 5 minutes longer and bake at 300 degrees.

Allow to cool before you refrigerate.

Top with sliced strawberries (optional)

Chocolate Peanut Butter Bites

If you like peanut butter cups, you'll love these!
My son Josh's favorites!

Ingredients:

¾ cup brown sugar

1 lb. powdered sugar

1 stick butter (softened)

2 cups peanut butter

2 cups unsalted peanuts

12 ounces semi sweet chocolate chips

1 T. sweet butter

Mix first 5 ingredients, pat into jellyroll pan. Flatten with rolling pin

Melt chocolate chips with 1 T. sweet butter in microwave

Spread on top of peanut butter layer

Cut into squares before refrigerating

Chill for at least 20 minutes, remove from pan and store in refrigerator.

Lemon Pound Cake

This is a delicious cake that I love to serve with breakfast.
It's so moist and not too sweet.

Combine:
1 Duncan Hines Yellow or Lemon Cake mix
1 package of lemon instant pudding (serves 4)
½ cup veggie oil
4 eggs

Put all ingredients in a bowl and beat for 2 minutes. Bake at 350 degrees in greased and floured Bundt pan for 45-55 minutes

Glaze (optional): 1 cup powdered sugar, 1 T. milk or lemon juice, 1 t. oil

Carole's Oatmeal Crunchy Cookies

Ingredients:
1 cup granulated white sugar
1 cup packed brown sugar
1 cup butter Crisco
Cream well
2 eggs (room temp) add one at a time
1 t. vanilla

Mix together:
2 cups all purpose flour
1 t. baking powder
1 t. baking soda
½ t. salt
Add to creamed sugar mixture

Stir in:
1 ½ cups quick oats
½ cup chopped pecans
Roll into one-inch balls. Dip tops of cookie ball into granulated sugar. Place on ungreased cookie sheet two inches apart. Bake in preheated oven at 375 degrees for 8-10 minutes depending on the crispness you like.

Renee's Outrageous White Chocolate Mousse

This is an easy, impressive dessert that will certainly please any guest, especially if you have friends who don't eat real chocolate.

Beat with electric mixer until fluffy:
2 cups heavy whipping cream
½ cup sugar
Set aside

In small microwave safe bowl, melt 6 blocks of Baker's white chocolate
In another bowl beat 6 oz. cream cheese, then add melted chocolate
After cream cheese and white chocolate are combined, fold in whipping cream by hand
Pour into dessert cups and top with raspberries, blueberries or fruit of your choice
Serves 8

A balanced diet is a cookie in each hand!

~ Barbara Johnson, author and comedian

Peanut Buster Pizza

Prepare 1 package Brownie mix (20-ounce size). Place parchment paper on a 15-inch baking stone. Pour prepared Brownie mix on the paper to form a 14-inch circle. *Do not attempt this recipe without the parchment paper or batter will run off stone!*

Immediately place in preheated 350-degree oven and bake for 20-25 minutes, then let cool completely.

Cream together:
1 cup (packed) brown sugar
1 package cream cheese (8 oz.)
¼ cup creamy peanut butter
Spread over cooled brownie circle.

Chop together:
¼ cup peanuts with 2 peanut butter cups (1.6 oz each)
Sprinkle over the peanut butter mixture.

Slice 2 bananas to arrange on top of brownie crust. *(Do this last as they brown quickly).* Set aside for topping

Topping:
Melt together in a microwave:
1 ounce semi-sweet chocolate square (2 T.)
2 t. butter

Drizzle "pizza" with melted chocolate and serve by cutting into squares.

Betty's Strawberry Parfait
Not only pretty, but really delicious!

Cut up 2 pint-size baskets of fresh strawberries
Combine with one carton of frozen strawberries
Cut one Angel Food Cake into small pieces
Prepare 1 quart of whipping cream, adding sugar

In a large glass bowl, start the layers with the cake, alternating the strawberries with the whipped cream…until all ingredients are finished.

Blueberry Crunch
Easy and delicious!

Layer the following:

1 can of crushed pineapple, (15 oz.) un-drained
1 package frozen or fresh blueberries (16 ounce)
¼ cup sugar
1 box yellow cake mix (dry)
¾ cup butter melted (1 ½ sticks)
¼ cup sugar
1 cup chopped nuts (preferably pecans)
⅓ cup flaked coconut

In a greased 9 x 13 baking pan, arrange ingredients in the following order:
Pineapple with juice, blueberries, ¼ cup sugar, dry cake mix, melted butter drizzled, ¼ cup sugar, chopped nuts and coconut. Bake at 325 degrees for 1 hour. Serve warm or cold with whipped cream or ice cream.

The Cake Lady's Butter-Cream Cake & Icing

Prepare:
Duncan Hines Butter Golden cake mix following directions except instead of butter
Use *Blue Bonnet* margarine

Icing:
1 cup Crisco
1 cup Blue Bonnet margarine
2 t. clear vanilla
2 lbs. powdered sugar
Mix with mixer and you can add up to 4 T. milk if too stiff.

For chocolate icing add ¾ cup Hershey's baking chocolate

I found this amount of icing to be too much if I'm doing a cake in an 11x13 inch-baking dish. But it kept well in the refrigerator and I used it a few days later for cupcakes. I think doing half the recipe would be perfect for that size cake.

What a treat to include this recipe from my long time friend, Carole, the baker. Carole's decorated cakes have always been at our family gatherings, including Beth and Josh's wedding. How very generous of her to allow me to print her recipe for, our all time favorite, butter cream cake and icing. I'm not sure if it was her signature basket weave icing that made it taste so good because it looked so beautiful, or if the taste was truly out of this world. Makes no difference, it was always our family favorite! I have always used Duncan Hines products but what a shock to learn, after all these years, her cake was a Duncan Hines box cake!

Pineapple Cake

I've served this cake for years! My guests rave about the taste, but never guess the ingredients. So easy! You don't even grease the baking dish.

Combine:
½ cup pecans chopped
1 can of can crushed pineapple with juice (20 oz.)
2 eggs beaten
2 cups sugar
2 cups flour
1 t. vanilla
2 t. baking soda

Mix together with a spoon. Pour into an un-greased 9 x 13 baking dish. Bake at 350 degrees for 35 to 45 minutes. After completely cooled, frost with cream cheese icing.

Cream Cheese Icing

Blend:
8 ounces of cream cheese, softened
1 stick butter softened
2 ½ cups powdered sugar
1 t. vanilla

Spread over cooled pineapple cake and refrigerate.

I just hate health food. ~ Julia Child

Franie's Dessert Crepes

Ingredients:
4 eggs
1 cup flour
2 T. Sugar
1 cup milk
¼ cup water
1 T. melted butter

With an electric mixer, beat eggs and sugar together before gradually adding flour and milk. Beat until mixture is smooth. Add melted butter. Set aside for not more than six hours at room temperature.

When ready to cook, batter should be as thin as heavy cream. Add a little milk if too thick.

Lightly oil a small, round frying pan skillet, heat pan to medium heat. (Six-inch skillet) Pour about 1/8 cup of batter into hot surface, using your wrist to spread batter evenly around the round surface. Cook only for a few seconds, or until edges begin to curl and crepe is golden brown. Place each crepe on a wire rack to cool, and then transfer onto wax paper.

Can be frozen by placing wax paper between each crepe.

When my good buddy Frances told me about making home-made crepes for manicotti, I jumped at the thought of learning this! Not only could these crepes be used for manicotti, but a few changes and they became dessert crepes as well. It wasn't generous enough that she gave me the recipe...she insisted that she would come over and coach me while I accomplished this cooking feat for the first time. Now that's a friend!

Johanna's Fruit Slush
So easy to make and super refreshing!

In a small saucepan, combine 2 cups sugar (or Spenda brand replacement to equal the sugar) with 2 cups water and bring to boil to dissolve sugar.

In a large bowl, combine the sugar water with the following ingredients and stir:
1 can frozen orange juice concentrate
18 oz. regular or diet 7-Up
20 oz. can of crushed pineapple with juice
2 cans Mandarin oranges (drained)
Grapes--any kind of seedless you choose
Maraschino cherries (with juice) about 1 to 2 jars. *You can also add bananas but they will brown.* Stir ingredients well before pouring into smaller plastic containers to freeze. Thaw slightly before serving.

Amanda's Easy Lemon Cheesecake
Quick and easy to prepare!

Ingredients:
1 package cream cheese (8 oz)
1 cup sugar
2 t. vanilla
1 package Dream Whip (prepare according to directions)
1 box lemon Jell-O (3 oz size)
9-inch Graham cracker piecrust

Prepare Jell-O according to directions and let cool until slightly thickened. Mix cream cheese, sugar and vanilla with electric mixer. Beat the thickened Jell-O with mixer before adding the Dream Whip and cheese combination. Pour over Graham cracker crust. Refrigerate until firm.

Something Special Layered Dessert

Crust: 2 sticks of butter, melted
2 cups flour
½ to 1 cup finely chopped unsalted pecans

Press into a 9 x13 glass pan and bake at 350 degrees for 12-15 minutes. Allow to completely cool before proceeding to next step.

1st layer:
Combine:
1 package cream cheese (8 oz)
1 cup powdered sugar
½ container of cool whip (16 oz)
Coconut (optional)

2nd layer:
2 boxes of instant pudding prepared (any flavor) (4 oz. size)
Bananas are optional on this layer.

3rd layer:
Remainder of Cool Whip garnished with coconut or sprinkled chopped nuts.

Stressed spelled backwards is desserts. Coincidence? I think not! ~ Anonymous

Helpful Hints
From
Susan aka Mimi

Granulated Garlic: *The Best! Garlic salt is too salty, garlic powder is a waste of time! My brother-in-law, Bob, owner of several great restaurants gave me this hint many years ago, he always used Granulated Garlic over any other processed garlic. They have it at Sam's Club, I've even found it at Odd Lots and of course, many Italian Delis. You'll not regret buying it, the flavor is as close to fresh as you'll find. Many times I combine it with fresh, putting both in a single recipe. If "garlic" is called for in any recipe other than cloves, I am using "granulated garlic."*

Crushed Red Pepper: *You'll notice that in many recipes I throw in crushed red pepper. It's become a staple in my kitchen! In the early years I really didn't care for the hot stuff, but after a trip to San Diego, California to visit Doc's parents, I started to change my mind. We often visited an Italian Restaurant on India Street called Flippi's Pizza Grotto and Deli (see them on the web) for pizza and meatballs the size of large grapefruit. It was then I started to order the red pepper to have it shipped to Ohio. This is not typical red pepper. It adds flavor without adding the super hot bite you get from most crushed red peppers. At Christmas our grown kids would often find Flippi's in their stockings. I now order it by the dozen and often bring it as a hostess gift when I'm invited to someone's home for dinner. It adds much flavor without the burn. Most people ask what gives that dish the "kick"; it's the crushed red pepper from Flippis.*

Garlic Press: *I have used them all! The number one, in my mind, is made by Kuhn Rikon. It's so easy to clean and it does the job beautifully. Also, a common gift for me to give a friend who loves to cook. Can be found at Williams-Sonoma, or if you're lucky, TJ Maxx or Home Goods.*

Spin Your Salad: *My special son-in-law, Brett, got me turned on to this. He is always the one to finish the salad.*

No matter how big I make it, there's never any leftover if Brett is here. When you add salad dressing to wet salad, you dilute the dressing and it's never as good. Spinning takes out the excess water. I spin extra lettuce, then bag it for use later.

Use Fresh Lettuce: *You will never find bagged lettuce in my refrigerator. (Well maybe if I'm out of town) I can always taste the chemicals. Friends call me the salad queen and it's partly due to the fact that I insist on* **fresh** *lettuce. You can make a salad early in the day and cover it with a slightly damp paper towel, until you serve it. Often I embarrass my kids by asking at a restaurant if the salad is bagged, if so, I refuse it. Another tip for keeping lettuce fresh is to wrap it in a damp dishtowel and put it back in the refrigerator. Invest in a good salad spinner!*

Salad Dressings: *I prefer homemade salad dressings. When you make a homemade dressing, it will keep in your refrigerator for weeks. So make it and have it with different combinations of veggies and lettuce. It will be well worth your time. My exception is Good Season Boxed Dressing where you add olive oil, red wine vinegar and garlic. See Italian Salad Dressing on page 47.*

Pasta: *I tend to buy Barilla pasta brand. Remember when choosing a noodle for your sauce, the heavier the sauce the larger the noodle. Always salt your water, but don't put oil in the water. Oil will make the pasta slick and your sauce won't stick to it as well. Many pasta casseroles will improve in flavor if it sits overnight. Therefore, make it a day ahead of time, save your time for last minute chores.*

Corn on the cob: *We love corn on the cob and in the summer it's so plentiful I've found that if I cook more than I think we'll eat, I get a lot of mileage out of it. First off, the grandkids love it from an early age, so they will eat more if*

163

it's cut off the cob. I keep it in the refrigerator and throw it on all kinds of dishes. With cooked down green beans/new potatoes it makes a wonderful veggie lunch. I put it on any tossed salad. I also add it to make up a quick bean salsa. Leftovers play a huge part in what we have for lunch, so I'm never afraid to make a little extra.

Fresh Basil: *Recently a friend taught me a trick about fresh basil that is truly worth sharing. In the summer I grow basil and we enjoy it in many of our dishes. It seems so sad that as fall approaches we have more basil than we can use and soon it won't be good. Here's what I do. Take fresh basil leaves and cut them (with scissors) in very tiny pieces, put them in a small glass jar and cover the basil with olive oil, making sure you have a tight lid. Store in the refrigerator and you can use it up to the time when we start to grow it again. Almost any recipe with basil will also use a little oil in it, so the extra oil from the basil shouldn't be a problem. Thanks, John and Lisa! Another hint about basil is that you can take a sprig and put it in a flower vase with water and put it into the refrigerator or let it set on your kitchen counter. I think it's just as pretty as a flower...now that's Italian.*

Onions: *For years we have stood in the kitchen and wanted a sure cure for peeling and dicing onions. I've heard run water while doing the dicing. That's ok but what about all the water we're wasting? I've also heard put a piece of bread in your mouth while cutting the onion, ok...but how silly do we look holding a piece of hot dog bun in our mouths? This is the best solution I've found. When cutting the onion position your cutting board on the stove near the vent and turn it on full blast. The aroma and strong vapors of the onion will be pulled out by the exhaust fan and you won't have onion tears in your eyes.*

Salting Chicken: *When preparing a chicken recipe, I often salt and refrigerate overnight, if possible. Sometimes*

I do this in the morning if am not able to do overnight. It tenderizes the meat. Many years ago I read a tip from a recipe from someone who won a "Best Fried Chicken" contest. The only difference in my recipe and the winner was the salting trick, so I adapted it to my chicken recipes. If you are trying to avoid too much salt, rinse and dry the chicken before you start to put the seasonings on.

Let's talk Phyllo Dough! *Fillo Dough (both spellings are correct) originally called Athens Strudel Leaves: In this cookbook, I've included several recipes that call for this dough. Years ago, an Armenian lady friend taught me how to make Baklava, which required working with this super thin dough. The best way to learn the techniques of phyllo is to watch someone work with it because there are lots of dos and don'ts. However, if you don't have a hands-on-experience, here are some hints acquired the hard way, which will save you a headache or two.*
*The dough is paper-thin. It comes frozen; so make sure you allow time to thaw according to directions on the box. Carefully unfold thawed stacks of the thin dough. After removing the first layer, cover remaining dough with a piece of damp cheesecloth, or damp paper towel. This means each time you get a new layer, you will uncover and recover it, it's laborious, but necessary. Always use melted butter liberally! Keep reheating the butter to keep it melted. I use a pastry brush to flick the butter on the dough. If you use a brushing action, you will need to be **very** light-handed, as the dough will easily tear.*
When your recipe is finished (i.e. cherry strudel) you will have a rolled up dough log. Always cut the dough BEFORE baking. With a sharp knife, cut just down to the last layer, but not all the way through. Cut according to the individual portion size you prefer. Warning: As with strudel, if you bake it before cutting, the dough will be so flaky that it falls apart when trying to cut into individual pieces.

The recipes I've included using fillo dough freeze well before baking. Before freezing, make sure you store it carefully (don't stack, as it crushes easily).

Make entertaining fun! *When entertaining I usually have a special theme in mind. When Don began teaching in a family practice program I was asked to host a party for the residents in our home. Since many of the future doctors represented various foreign homelands, I came up with the idea of an international party featuring foods from other countries. For that first potluck gathering, the invite was clear that each family be creative in the dish they brought to share. Some of the guys tried to weasel out of bringing an ethnic dish, so I suggested bringing a pizza cut in small pieces. They got the idea! Over the following 17 years that Don and I have hosted this annual event, we have enjoyed the most awesome array of dishes, not to mention the interesting stories behind every recipe. Sometimes a Mom of one of the residents will make his or her favorite dish to send. It's always delightful and the food is out of this world!*
I hosted a family birthday party for my dad towards the end of his battle with Alzheimer's. All my guests were required to wear a hat to grace my door. It was met with some resistance, but we all donned silly hats from the youngest to the oldest, which made Dad smile. That's what life is really about – loving and laughing and of course…eating delicious food prepared by hearts that care.

Tidbits About Susan

During a recent summer-long stay in Columbus from Cape Coral, I visited my Ohio friends, Don and Susan Furci. During my few days with them, the idea for this cookbook sprung from a recipe-conversation with Susie. In fact, a few months later, I'm still coming by to work on this enjoyable project as a tribute to a great cook and my dear friend of over thirty-five years. It's turned into Susan's cookbook memoir, so enjoy the "tidbits" about my friend taken from my book entitled "Puttin' On the Dog & Gettin' Bit."

In July, the first night of our visit, while talking about spaghetti pizza, a casserole I had never tried, Susan quickly fetched a three-ring binder containing most of her fabulous recipes. After leafing through it, I gushed, "Oh my gosh! I'm taking this to Kinko's tomorrow to copy every page." But the more I thought about her unusual collection of recipes; an actual cookbook presentation for family and friends seemed like a better idea! Before long I was on the computer creating a cover design proving how easy and rewarding self-publishing can be. Establishing this collection of recipes together with her has been a labor of love knowing the joy to come for all who often ask Susan to write a cookbook!

Earlier this summer, during a medical visit to Doc's family clinic, I was in the exam room with a resident treating me for laryngitis. Don came in to greet me with a hug and to introduce me to the attending doctor as "an author of books." I didn't get a chance to add that his wife was actually the *star* of one of my books—"Puttin' On the Dog"... my own memoir of sorts. Genuine people with flamboyant personalities are so much fun to write about!

Therefore, in keeping with this cooking theme, I'm calling Susan's seven chapters "tidbits." These tidbits are some infamous tales about the colorful and vivacious Susan that I couldn't resist putting into print. Since my friend and I both love entertaining and certainly "putting on the dog," we've had some amusing backlashes of getting bit! But it's all been worth every bite!

Enjoy!

www.barbarasanders.com

Pass the Charred Chicken Breasts!

Several years ago, *Gourmet Magazine* featured a glamorous glazed chicken arrangement on its June cover. It motivated me to amaze my friends at a 4th of July cookout, just to show off doing this very complicated recipe.

To save money, I skinned and de-boned ten whole chicken breasts. The exotic recipe called for expensive spices I had never heard of, so I raced across town to a specialty shop. The three separate sauces were prepared and cooked in advance. One cooked-down sauce was marinade for the chicken, one sauce was to glaze while slow cooking, and another sauce was to pass after the chicken was roasted to a golden brown. In addition, the breasts were stuffed with a minced pecan mixture and wrapped in bacon – a time-consuming preparation. If you count the de-boning, three separate, made-from-scratch, sauces and the two-hour drive time to buy the expensive, exotic spices, I spent about fifteen hours on this lone chicken recipe.

The stage was set: On the day of the cookout with friends, not leaving anything to chance, and knowing my husband wouldn't have the coals just right, I took matters into my own hands. Those under heated coals have been a bone of contention throughout our marriage. My "crowning moment" was to be the presentation of this glorious honey-glazed chicken dish featured on the cover of *Gourmet Magazine.* I fired up the coals in the outside grill about two hours before our guests arrived.

As we were ready to dine, Susan was standing next to me, tossing the salad. We were elbow-to-elbow at my kitchen island as I sliced up hot garlic bread with a very long, sharp, pointed knife. My husband was outside with the other male spouses, grilling the glorious marinated chicken breasts.

Suddenly, my husband barged back into the kitchen, talking in a loud, odd voice. Outstretched from his arms was the large white platter of chicken that I envisioned would look exactly like the June cover of *Gourmet Magazine.*

"You won't believe this," he began, eyeballs ablaze. "You can ask the guys if you don't believe me – honest to God, all I did was put the lid down for just thirty seconds! When I opened it back up, the chicken looked like this!" He was flushed from trying to explain.

He cautiously set the dish of grilled chicken on the counter in front of Susan and me. Every single, delicately bacon-wrapped chicken breast had been singed to a coal black ball of tar-like matter. The platter was adorned with what looked like an ensemble of charcoal briquettes.

My legs buckled. I gasped. I managed to suppress my urge to stab him with the long, pointed knife, which had remained suspended in midair. I had a sweeping desire to flee the room in tears to force our guests to evacuate. My jaw dropped. Those sweeping, surges of emotions took my breath away and left me completely mute. Susan broke the ice.

Leaning to my ear with a singsong voice, she whispered, "You know – the first one to *forgive* will get the blessing!"

I nearly turned the garlic bread-cutting knife on her.

Once we scraped the crusted chard off, the chicken was cooked well enough to eat. My huge regret was not taking a picture of the blackened dainties to send to the editors of *Gourmet Magazine* for the cover of their August issue!

The humbling, bumbling, burnt chicken mishap created an atmosphere of true confessions from the wives. Donna shared a nightmare about trying to impress her new neighbors with her culinary skills. One inspired summer day she drove out to a U-Pick-fruit farm in the country and picked two quarts of strawberries, one by one. That same day, pie dough was prepared with real butter, chilled, then artfully rolled out to fit in a brand new, over-sized, expensive Pyrex glass pie pan. The shell was baked and cooled, then filled with a yummy strawberry mixture made from the finest of ingredients.

The following day, Donna proudly presented the gorgeous pie with a "welcome-to-the-neighborhood" note, painstakingly written in calligraphy. The new neighbor, an absent-minded gynecologist, opened the front door to her smiling face. He reached out for the dazzling strawberry pie, thanked her, and then closed the door. Unfortunately, she never saw the whites of the eyes of the woman in the house.

About five weeks later, Donna bumped into one of the teenagers on the pathway leading to the lake. She greeted him with a friendly smile. "How did everyone enjoy the strawberry pie I made?" she asked, expecting a praise report.

"Oh, was that from *you*?" he asked, scratching his head before confessing. "Yesterday, Mom was cleaning out the fridge and found it way in the back. It really grossed her out 'cuz it was completely covered with black mold. She pitched the whole thing in the trashcan, pie plate and all. She wondered where it came from," he added with a chuckle.

Hearing that story, Susan seized the opportunity to get something off her chest.

"Well, that reminds *me* of the time I brought over my homemade cherry strudel and it landed in *your* trashcan!" Susan announced, glaring at me.

I sneaked a peek at my husband. He shrugged his shoulders. We both drew blanks, which only added insult to injury.

"Cherry strudel?" I smiled weakly, dumbfounded.

"How could you *not* remember?" Her bright hazel eyes were blazing. "It was Labor Day weekend, three years ago. I spent all day Friday making two large pans of cherry strudel. I brought the platters over on Saturday morning for your party on Monday. I told you, 'Now, this dessert, you can all eat right now, but don't let anyone touch this second platter. It's for the party.' My cherry strudel was missing at your party. Since I didn't save any strudel for us – I was really looking forward to having some…Remember! When I asked where it was, you said, 'Oh, Daryl and the kids started digging in to it with spoons. It got real gooey and messy in the pan, so I just threw it out.' Then you went digging around in the trash can and found the remains in the aluminum foil."

I knew better then to sing, *"The first one to forgive, gets the blessing."*

During that jarring journey down memory lane, I deeply regretted not schlepping a supermarket brand of cheap barbeque sauce over the chicken on my husband's ever loving, slow-start grill. So what if we had to wait another half hour for the coals to be ready? It would have been just as tasty. But then again, I wouldn't have heard Susan's need for therapy because her glorious cherry strudel came up missing from my buffet table three years earlier!

I'm finally learning that whenever I try to put on the dog, I always get bit!

Goodwill Misgiving

A few years ago, my friend Susan got the bright idea to volunteer as "the cook" for her husband's annual trip to Belize (formerly British Honduras). Dr. Don Furci is the current associate director of a large medical clinic in Columbus, Ohio. For the past fifteen years "Doc" has organized goodwill medical trips to this impoverished country. His dedicated team of fellow volunteer doctors and nurses take donated medical supplies on an exhaustive week long, free-clinic service to the needy.

For months before Susan's first and last trip to Belize, she enthusiastically emailed family and friends, rounding up delicious recipes to whip up to feed the entire mission team. She specifically asked me for a delicious breakfast casserole (recipe on page 104) made with browned sausage, which I have often served for company Sunday brunch. She carefully packed the sausage in dry ice and hand carried it on the airplane across the ocean for a breakfast debut.

Doc failed to enlighten his diva wife, a glamorous redhead, about the hazards and hellish living conditions for the natives in that country. Fortunately, a fellow team member, who had made morning coffee in that well-equipped kitchen on a previous trip, taught Susan to ward off hungry rats by banging dishpans on the exposed water pipes running down the kitchen wall. Since Susan and Don once served as medical missionaries in India, living in an orphanage, she wasn't as traumatized by the sight of a rodent.

Her husband's energetic medical team rushed off early each morning, passing up a big breakfast because the tropical heat was so unbearable. Susan's noble efforts ended up being more like confinement in a slave-labor camp.

Before arriving in Belize, Susan was instructed that there would be "additional kitchen helpers" from the town people. But for some unknown reason, there were no helping hands. All meal preparation, serving and cleanup, was left to Susan. The medical team was gone for more than ten hours each day, giving shots and dispensing medicines to mothers with very sick children. When the team returned each evening, they were close to collapsing from heat exhaustion and usually passed up eating her elaborate meals. So, how could she dare complain or request help from any of them?

One night, most likely out of guilt, the team finally surrendered to the elegant dinner Susan had prepared for them. While proudly dishing up the plates, she noticed that her husband was missing from the company that politely endured her long, five-course meal. Naturally, she inquired of his whereabouts.

"Doc went up to bed about an hour ago," replied the beleaguered colleague with a sheepish smile. Most likely Don ducked out to avoid the guilt offering Susan was finally getting to serve his heroic medical team.

Susan might have been on the brink of divorce by the end of that mission trip. Her stint on the mission field probably remains a sore subject with them, so I am reluctant to bring up the topic for any additional details. I am relying on my memory. As I recall, Doc was not amused, even though Susan attempted to be a good sport when relating the gory details to us during a dinner date.

But I do remember anxiously waiting for Susan's return. I couldn't wait to hear how the team enjoyed all of our delicious recipes. Unfortunately, this was another example of puttin' on the dog and gettin' bit!

Scandalously Clad Costume Party

My pal Susan is a gourmet cook, now infamous for her cherry strudel disaster and otherwise extravagant dinner parties. About thirty years ago she got the brainstorm to have a costume party in honor of Bea's birthday.

In her former and forsaken life, our friend, Bea, had been a dancing Rockette at the New York Radio City Music Hall. Purely for the shock value, Susan, the informant, loved to reveal this juicy tidbit of information because I only knew Bea as an ultra conservative, serious scholar, close to obtaining her doctorate at Ohio State University. For Bea's birthday party, the guest of honor was going to arrive dressed as a bumblebee, in a clever handmade black and yellow striped costume, complete with wings. Susan planned to wear all black, paint a white mask on her face like a mime and wear a pointed clown's hat. Don would rent a Civil War uniform. The other invited guests were not allowed entrance unless they were dressed in a costume.

Daryl and I had just been to Chicago for the *International Dance Festival.* I managed to drag my husband to *all six performances,* so I could lovingly gaze at Mikhail Baryshnikov, at the peak of his outstanding dance career.

"Hey, Daryl and I could come as *famous dancers.* We can dress him in leotards and he could come as Mikhail Baryshnikov and I'd be Margot Fontaine." *I was only kidding.*

Susan's face lit up with mischievous delight. "If you can talk him into doing that I will be *forever indebted* to you!" she cried in glee, begging me to follow through with the flamboyant notion.

Amazingly, Daryl agreed to don tights for the costume party. Making sure I wouldn't chicken out, Susan escorted me downtown to a dance-attire store to purchase the male ballet tights and to make *serious* inquiries about the under garments. After all, we didn't want my husband hanging out at the party.

"What do they wear under their … well, you know…is there a special jock strap?" I asked, feeling my cheeks flush.

Susan and I giggled like silly schoolgirls. The effeminate sales clerk was not at all amused, as he seriously explained the options of every male dancer while performing in tights.

My conservative husband, a former NFL offensive tackle, was talked into this crazy scheme. I think he did it just for Susan, knowing how delighted she would be to see him in drag.

At the time of the party, we were physically fit enough to pull off some smooth dance movements for the shrieking party crowd. Our *Pas de Deux* was a fitting tribute to Dr. Bea Edelstein, the former Rockette.

The Stork's Surprise Visit

On a Monday, a few months after the scandalous costume party, Bea and I arrived to help Susan prepare complicated appetizers for Bea's college graduation party on Friday. However, the famous party giver didn't anticipate the *early arrival* of her highly anticipated baby adoption that Monday!

Working with Phyllo dough can be tricky business because it's as thin as tissue paper. It quickly dries out and flakes, so the layers must be kept under damp dishtowels. The best of chef's have difficulty handling it. The Greek recipe was individual, one-inch squares of Phyllo dough, painted with melted butter, using a pastry brush, repeating the process three more times. Next, the buttered layers were topped with a dab of a cheese concoction, before quickly folding it in a perfect triangle to resemble a folded up American Flag. Susan could freeze them in advance. On the day of the party, she could pull them straight from the freezer to bake, turning out hot crispy golden brown delicacies to hungry guests.

Everything was going along smoothly until she discovered that Dr. Bea was not able to maneuver the dough properly. Like a military drill sergeant, Susan, hovered over us – moving back and forth from one table end to the other, inspecting every fold that our fingers managed. And she was not in the least bit diplomatic about correcting Bea's inept ability to fill and fold to perfection properly.

"I just can't get this technique -- I am all thumbs," said Bea with exasperated resolution. Not missing Susan's opportunity, Bea was banished to kitchen-cleanup by the commander-in-chief of the kitchen. There is no beating around the bush by Susan when it comes to cooking. After Bea was out of earshot, Susan looked at me and shook her head. "How can anyone *that smart* not catch on to something so simple?" I just smiled. Bea was in agony the entire time that she was attempting to master something as complicated as Phyllo dough. For Bea, the kitchen cleanup had to be a welcome relief from the peer pressure of dough-duty.

But in all fairness, that morning, Susan received a thrilling, but terrifying phone call that Bethany was born! As an inexperienced Mom, the expectant-adoptive-Mother to be was entitled to be a little edgy in the midst of the Phyllo-dough-demonstration.

In addition to preparing for Bea's grand graduation party that Friday, Susan had Bea's parents as houseguests. Susan had no baby furniture because the attorney advised them "not to purchase anything until the papers were signed." After the appetizers were finished, we zoomed off to buy baby furniture. While in the store, Susan reminded me "to stay focused" because I was off trying to purchase bags of play sand for my son's sandbox. But, on Wednesday, when newborn baby Bethany arrived, I was focused with my camera to capture another special moment with dear friends.

Susan's personal thoughts:

I never tire of hearing or telling this story of our Bethany. What a whirlwind it was welcoming our baby girl into our home. She brought such joy then and continues to enrich our lives daily. Her compassion and love for others is such a gift to our entire family. She's become a wonderful Mother, and we love spending time together with their three precious children; Abigail, Aiden and Sophia. I thank God for giving us Bethany and Joshua!

Passages of Life

After asking a stranger to lift a lone purple vase off the top shelf to place in my basket, I continued to mosey around house-wares in the upscale discount store. "Thank you, Sir." He smiled, but his wife gave me the evil eye.

As I turned the corner, our mini carts nearly collided in a kitchen aisle near an end cap containing stainless steel gadgets. The tall glamorous redhead looked like a movie star and slightly out of character in the discount department store. Rodeo Drive in Beverly Hills might be more appropriate for my dazzling friend who was golden brown from the sun, looking fabulous in an all white cotton jacket. Susan's polished nails were long and perfect. Nearly every finger was enhanced with her signature diamond rings – the only woman I know who might wear that many glistening baubles for breakfast each morning.

"Well, hello! What are you doing at my end of town?" I asked, grinning from ear to ear. Susan and Don Furci were our dearest friends, but it had been more than a year since we'd seen each other.

After hugging, Susan easily produced a painted wooden stick from her designer purse. It was tinted with soft pastels.

"I drove all the way over here to Burlington's trying to find a quilt to match this exact color for Abigail's new bed, but the store was *closed down!"*

"Oh, I know where their *new location* is. I just happened to see it yesterday. Oh, look at these *huge* garlic presses! Have you seen any like these?"

"Yes. And they really work *great*," Susan said, taking the press from my hands. "Look, see how this extra piece slides back and forth? The outer skin doesn't get stuck like the other presses. I'm buying two – one for our condo in Florida and another for a shower gift."

"Then I'll get one, too." I said. You can always count on Susan to be up on the latest of *everything*.

We continued discussing the baby's bedroom, picking up pace, as we headed toward the linen section of the store. Even though we had not seen each other for more than a year, there was no need for the usual *well, how have you been?* Or the awkward *what's new?* Time diminishes between old friends; therefore, we didn't miss a beat. No further explanations were necessary. It was if we had been traveling as a team all along, determined to find her soon-to-be-two, adorable granddaughter the perfect bedspread for her exalted departure from the crib.

"How's this one?" I asked, holding up a crib quilt in similar shades of purple and pink. I was thrilled to be part of the quest because watching Bethany grow up was very special to me. "Aunt" Barbara had been running the video when the adoption attorney handed three-day old baby Bethany into the anxious waiting arms of her new mother and father.

"That's nice, except it's a *crib cover*let. I need something slightly larger, but smaller than a day bed, and they're awfully hard to find."

Like determined birddogs on the trail of a pheasant, we drove on to the new *Burlington* store before finding the perfect lavender sheet and blanket set at *Baby's R Us* three hours later. Afterward, we caught up with each other's lives during a leisurely two-hour dinner.

Susan gave me a blow-by-blow account of the day on their Florida beach when her son, Josh, got engaged to Lena. I hung on every detail because I had known her children since birth.

To pop the question in a surprise to Lena, Josh requested *12 dozen* white roses under a rented, white tent set up on Siesta Key beach. Susan jumped into action and found 144 perfect white roses at a tremendous discount. She and her decorator friend pulled out all the stops with the perfect pieces to go inside the tent. They covered a table and two chairs in white, creating a romantic setting perfect for the prince and princess. Doc was dressed in a tuxedo ready to pour the champagne into stemmed glasses. " Not plastic ones, Mom. I want to hear the ting," Josh instructed.

Susan and the entire clan of kids were hiding in the bushes peeking out as the couple strolled up from the beach. As Josh and Lena walked down the beach to view the sunset, a crowd had gathered off in the distance waiting for the thrilling surprise to unfold. Many of the single women watching were swooning over the grand gesture by this handsome romantic.

"Oh, what's this?" Josh asked, as he steered Lena toward the extravagant setting. When they entered the tent, Lena cried when she saw her future father-in-law in a tuxedo, smiling brightly. She realized that the countless white roses and glowing candles were for *her* – a treasured moment to remember forever. Josh seated her. On bent knee, Josh presented his love with a diamond ring. The hovering beach crowd had moved in for a closer peek. They cheered when Lena said "yes."

The story brought tears to my eyes. A photographer captured the moment, and the *Sarasota News* broke the story, along with the photograph, which ran that weekend.

After our wonderful day together, Susan called a week later to invite Daryl and me to a private family gathering to celebrate Abby's second birthday. The last time I had seen Bethany's baby was at Don's mother's funeral nearly a year ago, some months before that, we celebrated her 95th birthday party.

It's been wonderful to have dear friends to experience so many passages of life together.

Susan's personal thoughts:

Speaking of that great day when our son Josh proposed, I would be remiss not to share a few thoughts about our daughter-in-law, Lena. As we write this book, she is expecting "grand one," number eight. You'll find several of her recipes included and I remember the first time she danced into my heart. It was Mother's Day when they were dating. I couldn't get over her confidence in wanting to cook dinner with Josh in my kitchen for our entire family. I knew she had heard many stories about me and my cooking. It didn't faze her in the least; she was in no way intimidated. I sat on a bar stool watching and advising them where to find all the necessary tools to prepare the meal.

I recall, as they dated, many friends heard me speak of my love for Lena, and warned, "You are going to be so disappointed if they don't marry!" They were right – I would have been crushed. But knowing how smart Josh is, I knew he wouldn't let this gem get away. So now, my blessing for all my girlfriends is that they would have a relationship with their own daughters-in-law like I have with my Lena. Common wisdom says there should be contention in that mother-wife relationship, but with God's help, I believe our in-laws can become a vibrant part of our families, and we can love them almost as much as we love our grown children. It can take a little work, but it's worth it for sure!

Surprises & Prizes

We arrived early, per Susan's request. "Please bring your camera and take some pictures of the baby before everyone gets here."

Dressed in bib overall shorts and barefoot, Susan was outside dashing toward the house next door. "Park over there!" She hollered, waving, smiling madly, and pointing to her neighbor's driveway. Even in bibs, she still looked glamorous.

As soon as Daryl and I stepped out of the car, Susan quickly guided us by the elbows through the neighbor's garage door, leading into the kitchen.

"Just take a whiff of that!" she said, beaming. The aroma of Italian chicken cooking in her neighbor's spare oven was intoxicating. We followed her to the stove. Opening the oven door, Susan proudly displayed four huge pans of baked chicken. A gesture so like Susan – getting tickled over a sneak preview of the delicious feast that had probably taken two whole days to prepare.

When we arrived back at Susan's house, the darling two-year-old birthday girl was in a princess dress with a red Binkie pressed to her lips.

"Oh, my goodness! I was there when your mom bought this dress! She looks so adorable in it!" I exclaimed to Bethany.

Bethany's handsome husband, Josh, was holding the baby, who looked very much like Bethany at that same age. Proud Papa was beaming.

In front of the fireplace, the tiny bed was the focal point, complete with the lavender bedding that Susan and I had sought like a hidden treasure. She had taken a weathered, brown wooden-spindled child's bed and transformed it with a coat of crème colored paint. The details were accented in an array of pastels – pink, lavender, green, and yellow. It was perfect. Bright, colorful batches of Helium balloons were attached to the headboard. The elaborate array of colorfully wrapped birthday gifts was gracefully displayed on the gorgeous lavender blanket. Stretched across the mantel were about twelve festive gift bags for all the cousins who would arrive later.

Two-year old Abigail kept saying she wanted to open her "prizes" (surprises) and began pulling tissue from one of her bright gift bags. The bed was a complete surprise to Bethany, who was thrilled by her mother's ability to transform something so plain into a true work of art.

The manicured back yard featured Don's newly updated rock waterfall and fishpond. I chuckled when I spotted a freestanding sign that boldly stated: "Thou Shalt Not Throw Rocks." On our unplanned Saturday outing, searching for the baby's bed quilting, Susan and I encountered a country craft store. We entered, hoping to find some homemade baby quilts in the right colors. Susan spotted the sign, which read something like *Welcome to my garden.* She bought it to repaint it, explaining why. Bailey, their other grandchild, is an adorable, but the rambunctious, nine-year old who had a blast throwing rocks in the water pond on her last visit. Unfortunately, the rubber water lining was punctured. But the replacement ended up being an elaborate update and a much more exotic water pond.

When we were shopping together earlier that month, Susan had two princess dresses draped from her basket when I returned from the rest room.

"Which one do you like better?" It was hard to decide – they were both fabulous. "Well, since I need two different sizes, I'll get one of each."

"Is the other one for our Bailey girl?"

"Are you kidding? Bailey would *never* wear a dress like this. This other one is for Taylor, the little girl next door."

Heidi, Don's beautiful and petite daughter from his first marriage, recently joined a *professional women's football team,* playing half back. Last week, Bailey's mother scored her first touchdown to a cheering crowd of proud parents and friends. Don chuckled when he said Heidi's friends started chanting "Heidi! Heidi!" after the Notre Dame movie called "Rudy." I thought they were pulling my leg until I saw pictures of Heidi in an actual football uniform, number 81, complete with a helmet and shoulder pads. Sunday was certainly full of surprises.

Susan's personal thoughts:

I felt both honored and blessed to take turns caring for our first grand baby, Bailey, for a few years while Heidi worked full time. It was a joy to see both of them a couple days a week, and Don and I loved having that time to bond with our sweet grandchild. Now as a teenager, Bailey girl is blossoming into a lovely young lady and has a wonderful brother, Brady, who lights up our lives as well.

Don't Get Caught In The Act!

Susan's dad was in the advance stages of Alzheimer disease. At her daughter, Bethany's baby shower, two years earlier, Susan's sister, Cathy, and her two sister-in-laws were seated with me, while we ate in the dining room. They began explaining Dad's recent admission to a nursing home and the adventures that soon developed after he arrived. Their dad began asking to "go home," expressing a renewed interest in romance with their mother, who hasn't received that much attention from him in over two decades! Feeling sorry for her dad, Cathy coaxed, "Mom, when he gets home…just take him in the bedroom, if he wants to go…."

At Abby's birthday party, I shared an intimate moment with Susan's parents after I ventured over to snap their photograph. Susan had rounded everyone up on their lush green lawn, for three-legged races, followed by a water balloon toss between parent and child. Susan was in her glory as the game captain, shouting out orders to her two brothers, Ed and John, their wives, Cathy, her sister, and all her nieces and nephews. The only thing missing was a whistle around her neck. Her parents were seated in the shade of a towering tree, holding hands under the pines, proudly watching their very healthy and active family enjoy life.

When I walked over to them with my camera, Mrs. Harris was now standing in front of her husband of more than 55 years. She held his hands, extended out like a child learning to "dance." Gone was the blank, distant stare from her husband's eyes. She was lovingly gazing into her husband's face, and he was grinning back at her. They were swaying as she held his outstretched hands, dancing as she sang every word to "Let me call you sweetheart…." From a respectful distance, I was privileged to share this sacred moment between them. The nurses had taught him to dance. In his early years he was very handsome and quite a ladies' man. For one passing moment, he was still that handsome guy. It was a precious moment between two sweethearts that I will never forget.

Did I mention Susan's delicious food buffet? Unfortunately, I was only on week two of the South Beach Diet that Susan raved about during our long dinner conversation. Motivated by all her weight-loss testimonies of friends, who lost big-time, I started the next day. After a 9 ½ pound weight loss in the first two weeks, I was determined not to cheat. But, boy was I tempted by Susan's elaborate buffet. There was corn pudding casserole, rave review pasta salad (*my* recipe, but tweaked by Susan), deviled eggs, fruit-salad, cooked-down green beans, Don's secret-marinade sliced flank steak, Italian style chicken (my husband instructed me to get the recipe) and for the dieters – sugar free Jell-O salad, that no one ate, including me.

There was, of course, a beautifully frosted and scrumptious butter cream sheet cake (so everyone said) topped with a *Number Two* candle. I noticed that someone cut a piece of the cake before the candle was lit and presented to Abigail. Fortunately for them, Susan didn't catch them in the act!

Susan's personal thoughts:

I've found the process of writing this book has brought back many poignant memories. As I reflect on the fun we had that day, I am also reminded of the loss of our father. Actually, it was loosing Dad that stirred me to write for the very first time. Once again, it was my friend, Barbara, who encouraged me to put my thoughts down on paper and I was privileged to read this tribute about my dad at his funeral.

Did You Know My Dad?

Sometimes I wonder did I really know you? All those years we spent together under the same roof and then my years as an adult, but who were you really? You were such a hard worker, never missed a day of work that I can remember. We used to look at that old photograph of that huge pile of equipment and I was convinced you moved it single handedly. To me, you were the strongest man on earth.

Yes, I admired your strength, but I secretly longed to see your softer side. A Daddy who would take me in your arms and hug me while telling me how very special I was to you. Instead, always in your teasing, playful manner, pushing me away, not knowing how to deal with my physical love towards you.

I didn't understand why you weren't able to give me the affection I so desperately needed. It wasn't until my early twenties that it started to make sense to me. It was all a part of your integrity and who you were. No one ever taught you how to show love. As a Father, you had no idea of the importance of showing physical love, or expressing your feelings. I'm so thankful that years ago, we overcame those obstacles. And that before the end came, you were totally **free**. Free to not only except, but to give physical love, to say those words, "I love you." Not only to me, but to all those who loved you.

I realize now how many fathers of your era were bound by the inability of touching and giving love in the ways children understand. You and yours believed, and rightly so, that going to work everyday and doing the best you could to supply us with the necessary items to make life good were the ways you showed love. I thank-you—we all thank-you for all you gave to and did for us.

Did You Know My dad?

If you were a young boy wanting to play baseball, you might have known him. He was a serious coach. He wanted to teach you to give your all, do your best and be a good winner but also an honorable loser. He spent many years giving of himself to help young men learn the sport but also to incorporate the values learned on the field for living life. If you were one of the lucky ones, I'm sure you would remember him.

If you were one of his golfing buddies chances are you learned from him also. He took his sports so seriously, but he knew how to have fun. The rules were always important to him, and he walked like a true champion. Winning his flight at Brookside Country Club Invitational proved it. He was just a country guy from Grove City, but he showed the big dogs how to play the game on their own turf. It was a thrill he shared with my husband, Don. Their golf triumph always brought smiles to their faces as they relived the details of that sweet victory they would never forget.

Have You Seen My Dad?

Somehow a terrible stranger slipped in, like a thief in the night, to carry my Dad away from us. We don't know how it happened but one day we started to notice that he's in another place, a place where we just can't reach him. He's changing, he's just not himself anymore. It's not that it's all bad there, just different. Like the day we rode in the back of the pickup together. We were suddenly like two kids laying down watching the sky, giggling and naming the images of the clouds as my brother drove us through the country roads. Laughing, feeling so adventurous, wondering if the "cops" were behind us, or could see us. Obviously, breaking the rules of safety, an act that would not have been tolerated by my dad. Somehow this new person was willing to break the rules, get a little closer to the edge, living life as never before. Something we could have never done if the stranger hadn't come.

Since the stranger came, it took my Dad further away every year. From caretakers, to hospitals, each journey went deeper into the unknown. Seeing his smile when I entered the room was always such a comfort to me. He knew me. Then, even that was gone. His journey had taken him to a place where he couldn't find me. I wondered, does he really recognize me, but is so held captive that he just can't express what is inside of him?

Do I See My Dad?

Absolutely. Whenever I see my brother John, coaching his son, back on the same diamonds where my dad spent so many years. Or when I see my brother Ed mowing and working at the farm. They can't help having his same body language, nor would they want it any other way.

When I see his family sons and daughters, grandchildren of all ages displaying his character, integrity, honesty, and a superior work ethic. Yes, I see my dad. When I look in the mirror and see all he gave me. He taught me to write in the book inside my heart The Rules to Live My Life By, yes, I see my dad. Was he perfect? No, but he's forgiven. I know that though he is gone from this life we will see him again and that will be a wonderful day, when we once again see our dad. We'll kiss him and hug his neck and tell him how much we missed him and then hear him say how he loved and missed us too.

*   *   *

As I read this at the funeral I heard my sister Cathy quietly weeping. I knew if I looked at her I'd loose it, so I managed to keep my composure. When I finished reading my younger brother, John, was standing to wrap his arms around me. He tearfully whispered, "You wrote this just for me." Then our other siblings, Ed and Cathy, joined us in a very tearful group hug. It was a tremendous release of emotions that we all had been carrying throughout our dad's long illness. I will never forget that moment.

Ingredients For a Happy Marriage

When you love someone, you are willing to give for them, and give up for them, and give in for them. ~ David Jeremiah

From Susan's Pen

"So, How Many Years Have We Been Married Now?"

"Good morning, Honey, do you know what today is?" Don spoke cheerfully while rousting me out of bed on February 9th, 2008. Without looking I knew his eyes were twinkling.

"Well, I think it's our anniversary," I mumbled, trying to awaken. My eyes were not yet open, and it was far too early in the morning to be jarred awake with a quiz.

"So, how many years has it been anyway?" I asked, stretching and peeking one eye open to catch my husband's reaction to my nonchalant attitude.

"You mean you really don't know?" he asked, looking bewildered at my lack of sentiment.

My sweet, sappy husband knew how long, to the very to the hour, we've been married, so I just had to tease him. Of course I knew the exact number of years, but I couldn't resist the opportunity to pull his chain. A trait I had mastered over the years, much to his dismay.

What a wonderful way to start our day, sipping our coffee on the lanai and watching the sunrise together. Soon, Don began reminiscing about our years together. And once again, my thoughts were swept away by our love story and how it all began thirty-four years earlier.

The late sixties ended a decade of change for both of us. We met after each of us came through heartbreaking, failed relationships. Don was halting a not-so-successful marriage that finally ended after years of heroic attempts to save it for the sake of his two children. Deeply troubled that his family was torn apart, naturally, as a good father, Don was worried about his children's future. If he went his own way, he didn't know what would happen to his kids. My life was just as uncertain. After a long-term relationship ended with a painful breakup, I was attempting to figure out where life would lead me. We both were searching for something meaningful in life, but it didn't seem within our grasp. The sun quit shining. We were aimlessly going through the motions of life when a ray of hope broke through the futile darkness.

The Magic begins:

As fate would have it, we met face-to-face in the hospital of all locations. Ironically, we both needed fixing, so what better place to begin an emotional healing process that neither of us recognized we needed.

After becoming gravely ill, I was admitted to the hospital where Don was on staff. Being a devoted doctor and very charming to his patients, he had been voted "Intern of the

Year" before finishing his residency there. Don's best friend, Frank, was my surgeon during a life-threatening operation. Since I made such a miraculous turn around after being close to death, my proud surgeon paraded other hospital staff in to greet his prize patient. My Aunt Jean, who had an exceptional flair for fashion, decked me out in a gorgeous, bright pink pajama ensemble with ruffles all across the bodice. I was dolled up in this knockout attire when Frank brought Don in to meet me. Little did I know what a "shocking pink" impression I made on the man who would later become the love of my life!

As Don recalls, the holidays during his stressful seven-year marriage were always difficult. However, since I had never married, and I had been living the carefree, good life, my holidays were great. Working downtown, as a popular barber, in an upscale salon, I looked forward to downtown celebrations with my favorite customers and fellow employees. For a little holiday shopping, during a lunch break, I'd often scurry across High Street to Lazarus, Columbus's finest fashion store. On one such Christmas shopping spree, as I scooted through the festive, holiday decorated department store, Don was answering a page at a pay phone near the entrance to the store. Don recognized me as I scurried by, but I didn't notice him observing me.

During this time frame, my cousin, a physician, had just returned home from Vietnam. We corresponded during his time away, so it was a thrill knowing that he was going to set up practice in the Columbus area. Not only would we be able to party together, but also I would have a "Doc" in the family. When the dreaded flu season hit, I found myself in desperate need of a good doctor. Since he was my cousin, I thought he would just phone a prescription in for me, so I was surely disappointed that he required an exam before writing a prescription. Feeling poorly, I drove to his office for my appointment. Little did I know that another key piece of our puzzle was about to be revealed. A nurse guided me to an exam room. As I waited on the table, a cute Italian doctor walked past my exam room. I suddenly realized it was the same attractive doctor I met while hospitalized a few years earlier. Since there were other Italians in my cousin's practice, I wasn't sure what his name was, but I knew it was *him*. This time, Don did not realize that I was now the one observing him.

The swank Columbus barbershop I worked in was downtown's finest. I felt fortunate to land a job in a posh place that served some of the most influential people in town. I also broke ground as one of the first female barbers in the city. Wearing sexy, miniskirts added to the allure of "Susie, the Barber." Yes, it was a great time for me! Don first came to our shop through Carole, our manicurist. Her brother, Eddie, was Don's barber, at another shop. Whenever Eddie was on vacation Don went to Bobbie, the barber in the chair next to me. Then, one fine day, both Eddie and Bobbie were on vacation...but, before I go there, I must tell you another important part of this story. It is about the day I visited my surgeon for my annual check-up.

As most women would agree, an annual exam is something we dread, but I had to go. After my exam, I was seated in my doctor's private office to talk about my medical issues. By divine appointment, his secretary buzzed in, "Dr. Furci is on line two." By this time I knew a little more about Dr. Don Furci because he came into the barbershop on occasion. In the past I found him attractive, but he was married and besides, I was also in a relationship. However, time had passed by and I was now a single lady. To my surprise, my physician, Frank, was expressing sympathy to Don regarding his recent separation. As Frank wrote down Don's new unlisted phone numbers, he repeated them back to him for clarity. Feeling awkward about overhearing this private phone conversation between two friends, I was, nonetheless, privy to personal information I might not have ever known otherwise. Years later, I would marvel at how slim the odds were that I would be seated in my doctor's office to overhear a very short, but vital conversation that completely changed the course of my life!

So, when Don called our shop to make a hair cut appointment, he got me since Eddie and Bobbie were both on vacation! As I clipped away at Don's hair, we made small talk. I mentioned that I had recently been in Frank's office the day he called with his new unlisted telephone numbers. Flirtatiously, I told Don I tried to remember the numbers, but by the time I got to the car, I had forgotten them. Don blushed when he smiled, but it appeared he didn't pick up the hint that I was interested in him. He paid for his hair cut and left without a word. This was long before cell phones, but to my amazement, the minute he returned to his office he picked up the phone to call me. His line was classic and unforgettable, "If you were serious about wanting my number, I'll give it to you over dinner."

During our first romantic dinner date, we had a delightful time recalling how many times our paths crossed over the previous four years. To my amazement, Don described those flamboyant pink pajamas with total recall, ruffles and all. He also revealed that he spotted "the tall, gorgeous red-head dashing through the department store as a breath of fresh air." He confessed that he felt despondent because of the holiday blues. He said, "You were so full of life. I knew if I could sit down and talk to you over lunch, you'd make me feel better." But at that time he was still married and it wouldn't have been appropriate. We laughed about me getting the flu and being in the *right place* just as he walked by my exam room. We now realize that God's timing is perfect. We were both ready when our lives were brought together after an extended time of needed separation to build a solid life together.

Although my husband probably wishes that I still wore racy ruffles to bed, and my tresses are no longer the sexy Farrah Fawcett hairstyle, and I always get my annual flu shot, he still considers me his "breath of fresh air." We still have candle lit, romantic dinners and laugh with each other often. Our life, as one, found true meaning. Together, we had another daughter and son, who are both grown and happily married to terrific spouses.

The holidays remain a true joy with four grown kids and precious grandchildren that keep us young and on our toes. We smile, we laugh and sometimes nudge each other with the question, "Only thirty-four-years?"

Susan's personal thoughts:

The ingredients for a happy marriage are laughter, commitment to each other, honoring God and each other, praying together, gratitude and a willingness to serve each other unselfishly. I can't say that we do this all the time, but we sure do try.

When Barbara encouraged me to start writing, this is one of the first attempts to record something important in my life. Since this cookbook has become a memoir, I'm passing this little bit of history on to our children and their children for posterity sake. I hope they'll appreciate hearing once again how their father and I met and fell in love.

Susan and Don, 2012

Recipe Index

Thank you, Anthony, for developing this great looking index!

We can complain because rose bushes have thorns, or rejoice because thorn bushes have roses. ~ Abraham Lincoln